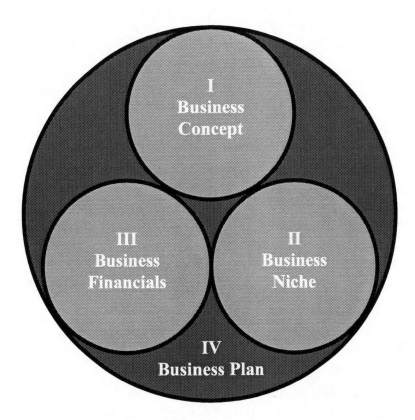

Disclaimer

The author has attempted to ensure that the information in this book is accurate but nothing herein should be interpreted as giving legal, tax or accounting advice. Professional assistance in these areas is recommended.

ISBN 0-7414-1578-X

Published by:

PUBLISHING.COM

519 West Lancaster Avenue
Haverford, PA 19041-1413
Info@buybooksontheweb.com
www.buybooksontheweb.com
Toll-free (877) BUY BOOK
Local Phone (610) 520-2500
Fax (610) 519-0261

∞

Printed in the United States of America

Printed on Recycled Paper

Published October 2003

Thoughts

This guide is for the somewhat inexperienced entrepreneur who needs help deciding if a business concept is viable and if so, how to get started on the right foot. It doesn't attempt to teach "everything you will ever need to know" about all aspects of business. It does cover the basic elements involved in evaluating the business opportunity and getting started. It also may help you decide that your idea is too risky to warrant investing your time, energy and financial resources at this time. If so, reaching this decision is also a valuable and valid outcome of the process.

Most small businesses start with one or perhaps two owner/operators. This small business model is the backbone of employment growth in the United States. In fact, as people are displaced from their regular employment as a result of downsizing and consolidation, a fair number use the opportunity to establish their own businesses. Many of the people I counsel fall into this group. They are well grounded in their fields and come with a high level of motivation and desire to succeed.

The structure of this guide is to present information, ideas and tools in a systematic manner, followed by the opportunity to apply them using model worksheets. Chapters are designed to combine topics that have strong business relationships. They are short enough to read, digest and apply quickly. The margins are wide so that you can make notes as thoughts occur to you. I want the essentials to be prominent and easy to understand. In a small business, "focus is crucial" and "less is often better".

A word about the cover. I used the picture of the Statue of Liberty on the cover because it is the symbol that I think best represents freedom and opportunity in the United States. These are the two critical constitutional rights that permit and encourage small businesses to form, grow and be successful. I hope that everyone recognizes how important these rights are to the continuation of our way of life.

Thank you for your interest in my book and good luck in your endeavor! I'd like to hear from you. My website address is on the back page.

Dick

Table of Contents

Overview

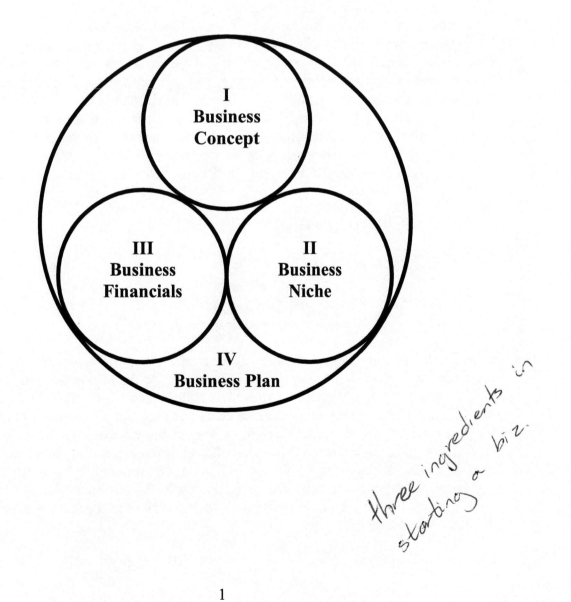

I
Business
Concept

III
Business
Financials

II
Business
Niche

IV
Business Plan

three ingredients in starting a biz.

<table>
<tr><td>

The Business Planning Process

</td><td>

</td></tr>
</table>

Introduction

Thinking about starting your own business is both exciting and scary. One of the objectives of this guide is to help you sustain the feelings of excitement while dispelling some of the fear. Starting a new business is a daunting task for the typical entrepreneur. Often there are so many questions and unknowns that they cloud the business vision and concept, perhaps convincing the emerging entrepreneur to give up the idea prematurely. The purpose of this book is to *provide both basic business information and a process for applying business principles* in an orderly, understandable way. Certainly, there will be areas that require additional research and learning beyond the scope of this book. However, it is more logical to describe a typical small business environment and its concerns, than it is to try and teach a multitude of complex topics that probably will not be encountered in the first few years of the business. For the purposes of this guide, a small business is defined as a one to four- person endeavor. This size covers 90% of the startup businesses in the United States.

Goals for this Guide

This guide has two goals:

- Teach you what you **need to know and do** to start a small business.
- Teach you **how to develop a basic business plan.**

These are not unrelated goals. You can't write a viable business plan without having some basic business knowledge. At the same time, you need a business plan to validate your business concept and to provide a road map for the first six to twelve months. In using this guide, you will see that basic business issues are discussed in a systematic manner. The data and decisions resulting from a discussion of these issues are directly transferable to a business plan format. If this guide is successful in helping you achieve these goals, you will be in a better position to realistically evaluate the true business opportunity and determine the desirability of proceeding with your business initiative.

Starting a Small Business

With these thoughts in mind, this guide incorporates the following concepts:

- Introduces business information in a top-down sequence. Starting at the business concept level and working down through greater levels of detail to the formal business plan.
- Presents information in logical groups or "packages" that relate to each other.
- Incorporates three, single-page worksheet models as an easy way to summarize and consolidate business information and decisions.
- Incorporates the creation of a "fictitious business" as the material is presented to demonstrate the application of the models and the business plan elements.
- Uses a table of contents for the business plan that mirrors the content and sequence of the information from the worksheet models.
- Uses plain business language and simple arithmetic.
- Establishes a learning and planning process that can be applied to the startup of any small business. This permits the learning to be reapplied to other new business opportunities if the initial idea is not viable.

Applying the Concepts

Let's talk about what to expect in using this guide. First of all, if you are new to the business world, you probably have a lot to learn. The trick with most learning in the business world is to learn what you need to know before you need to apply it. In the academic world, knowledge may be pursued for knowledge's sake, or to prepare for a non-specific future. However, securing "knowledge for knowledge's sake" is a luxury that most entrepreneurs cannot afford. At the same time, they must learn what they need to know in time to stay out of trouble and make good decisions.

That's what this guide tries to deliver - knowledge delivered "just-in-time" to make the right decisions and to expose any topics that require additional research. For this learning system to work best, the user should have a target business idea or concept in mind. If that is not the case, it is best to apply the principles to a fictitious business idea to realize the full value of the worksheets and business plan format.

One more word in this area - as an entrepreneur, you may think that you don't have a lot of time to devote to learning. Yet, to be a successful small business owner, you must always be learning because you must wear many hats. Embrace continued learning - it's one of the keys to entrepreneurial success!

Starting a Small Business

The Planning Process has Four Parts

This guide is divided into four parts that correspond to the four major steps in the planning process. It is designed to lead you progressively through three levels of business analysis and planning before finalizing the business plan in Part 4. Each of the first three levels has a different purpose and a different level of detail - from less to more. The topics within each group also have a synergy - they relate closely and are usually dependent upon each other. They are designed to provide a concentrated view of an important aspect of the business.

The graphic on the preceding Overview page portrays these concepts and components. As we go through the process we will fill in the graphic one major component at a time. When the process is complete the graphic will be completely filled in. Let's preview each of the four parts and the tools we use to establish order and define relationships. Then you will understand how the guide is structured and how to benefit from each step in the process.

Part I: Business Concept - A High-Level View

We start the process by describing the broad basic characteristics of the business using a one-page Concept Model composed of five topics:

1. Business Concept
2. Market Opportunity
3. Legal form and ownership of the business
4. Owner's goals
5. Strategies that will drive attainment of the goals

Completion of the Concept Model will confirm that you have a well thought-out and documented high-level view of the business and that you are ready to move to the next step. Inability to complete this model suggests that you may still have basic research or decision-making tasks to complete. Chapters 1 through 4 cover the materials that are relevant to completion of this model. When the Concept Model is completed, you may be surprised at how well it describes your target business. Also, do not be surprised if your view of the business opportunity changes somewhat as you drive down the level of detail in the subsequent models. As you will see later, the topics covered in the Concept Model are directly transferable to the business plan.

Part II: Business Niche - A Mid-Level View

The purpose of the Niche Model is to focus on the five core elements of all businesses and establish their specific characteristics for your business. These five elements are alluded to in the Concept Model. This is the opportunity to define them in more detail and make sure you fully understand their relationships.

these 5 areas must work well together.

The five elements of the Niche Model are:
1. Your products and services
2. Your ideal customer profiles
3. Basis for your pricing policy
4. Your competition and competitive edge
5. Your marketing, advertising and sales approach

The Niche Model is the tool that forces you to consider these five elements individually, and in relationship to each other. They establish an important business context. The elements must be fully understood and balanced with each other to produce an effective business configuration. In fact, you may need to complete more than one version of the model to capture different product/service and customer profile variations. Information from this model transfers directly to corresponding sections of the business plan. Chapters 5 through 8 cover the materials relevant to the completion of this model.

Part III: Business Financials - A Detailed View

The greatest level of detail always occurs in the financial projections. Financial projections require that planned business activities be converted into *detailed monthly projections* for a two or three-year period. The validity of these financial projections is dependent upon the accuracy of the assumptions used in their preparation. That is the reason that financial projections are the final phase in the business planning sequence. You need the source information from the Concept Model and the Niche Model to create the assumptions that underlie the financial projections. Too often in planning, the financial projections are completed first and the business is forced into that financial mold. Later someone wonders why things didn't turn out as projected. Making financial projections is always risky. It is even more risky if it is not based on sound facts and realistic assumptions.

The Financial Model contains the following five types of information:

1. Sales projections by product/service, price and volume
2. Gross Income
3. Cost of Goods
4. Expenses
5. Net Profit (or Loss)

Other essential financial reports are also covered, including Startup Expenses, Balance Sheet and the Cash Flow Statement. Chapters 9 through 11 cover the relevant financial topics.

Part IV: Business Plan - The TechServ Story

A fictitious small business is used to illustrate application of the various elements of the planning process. The business, named TechServ, LLC, is introduced in Chapter 1. The three planning models and other financial reports for this business are populated at the appropriate points during the process. Part IV contains a sample business plan for TechServ that was created from the information extracted from these worksheets. This sample demonstrates how easy it is to extrapolate worksheet data into a comprehensive business plan.

Part I:

Business Concept

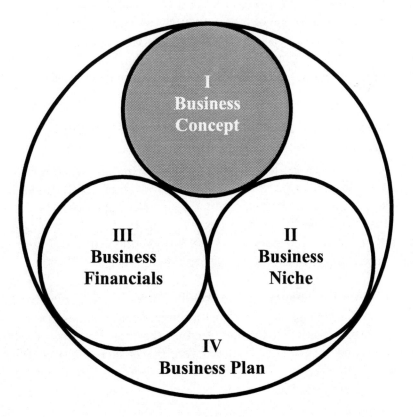

<table>
<tr><td>

Starting to Define the Business

</td><td>

1

</td></tr>
</table>

Introduction

We learn more about business if the learning takes place in relation to a real-life situation, rather than in a theoretical context. Business ventures, like other life experiences, involve making serious choices. Weighing alternatives, making decisions and deciding relative importance (prioritization) are the daily bread for the entrepreneur. To maximize the value of this guide, it is best if you have a real business application under consideration. In the absence of a real business situation, it is recommended that you select a test business for learning purposes. This will provide the opportunity to use the model worksheets and the business plan outline, which are fundamental parts of this "learning and doing" technique.

The Top-Down Approach to Business Planning

Research and experience have proven that business planning is more effective if the broad concepts of a business venture are defined before getting bogged down with too much detail. This approach is typically referred to as "top-down planning". It starts with the broad perspective and general outline of the business and then works down through successive levels of detail. That is the approach used in this guide.

The practical tool for developing the broad outlines for this top-down view is the Concept Model that summarizes the significant business elements in abbreviated form. Chapters 1 through 4 cover the topic material required to complete the Concept Model. Each of five major elements occupies one portion of the worksheet. The worksheet can be completed in your own handwriting and modified as learning and decision-making progresses. This is not a course in developing writing skills. The intent here is to use the model to present your ideas in a coherent form that will stand the test of logic and judgment.

The Concept Model

There is a blank Concept Model form for your use in the Appendix. A sample worksheet for our fictitious company TechServ appears at the end of this chapter. Let's review the content of the five sections of the model:

1. Business Concept - a short (5 sentences or less) description of the business concept.
2. Market Opportunity - a short (5 sentences or less) description of the market opportunity.
3. Owner information (including legal form).
4. Goals - one-sentence description for each of the three most important goals.
5. Strategies - a brief description of the strategies that will be used to achieve each goal.

Note: Try to limit yourself to this single page for capturing the information. It forces you to reduce the ideas to their essence, and is helpful in illuminating basic relationships and evaluating the relative merits of each component.

Please complete your own Concept model as you work through the material in these chapters. You may find that you need to do more research before reaching final decisions on everything, but it is helpful to establish a written baseline position for comparing alternatives and identifying outstanding issues.

Defining the Business Concept

The first step in business planning is to define the concept behind your business idea. Everything that follows will be tested against this initial basic business concept. You will see a natural progression of topics, research and decision-making evolve from this business definition. It is also likely that you will make some modifications to the initial concept as various business factors are applied.

The description of the business concept, as part of the Concept Model, is a concise description of the basic nature of the business under consideration. The business concept is the "essence" of the proposed business. There will be time and space to elaborate on the details later in the business plan.

Sometimes a business concept definition starts with what sounds like many other businesses but then becomes different because of some unusual feature. Let me give you two examples from a recent class. A lady said her business concept was to start a hair and beauty products home-delivery business. There are many similar businesses in the area but her business was going to be different because she had access to a high quality line of imported products that were not available in her market area. As a high-end supplier, she felt there were many customers available to her whose needs were not being met by other suppliers. The second example concerned a young man that was going to open a picture framing business. He had started on a part-time basis so he had a small established clientele. More importantly, he was trained as an artist and he felt he could offer more professional advice regarding mat coloring and frame coordination. He also would have a greater opportunity to sell his own paintings. He felt all of these factors would provide some competitive advantage. So, the point is that you don't have to have a completely new idea to be successful but it may help if you have some unique characteristics. We will talk about this more when we discuss competitive edge.

The essence of the business concept may include brief comments on the following topics:

- Is this a product-based business, a service-based business, or both?
- What are the general types of products or services to be offered?
- Are the products or services unique in any way?
- Are the primary customers businesses, consumers, or both?
- Is the business geographically constrained?
- What is the primary business function - manufacturing, wholesale, retail, etc.?
- Does the owner have experience in this business segment?

Brief answers to these questions are meant to serve as an introduction to the business and its owner. If prepared carefully, this brief description will permit any reader to quickly have a sense of the basic nature of this business. No more than five sentences should be used in this description.

Defining the Market Opportunity

The same rules apply to defining the market opportunity. Only the subject matter is changed. The market opportunity description explains why there is a need for these products or services and why there is "space" in the marketplace for this business to be successful. It should be a layman's description of the opportunity, not a marketing plan. The level of detail for a marketing plan can be included in the formal business plan.

The two examples described above include an indication of a confirmed unmet need in the marketplace. Remember, the business concept describes the nature of the business while the market opportunity describes the market conditions that support why this concept has a reasonable chance of success by satisfying an existing customer need.

The essence of the perceived market opportunity may include brief comments on the following topics:

- What are the "unmet or unsatisfied" customer needs that have been identified? *or competitive edge. or*
- What products or services will satisfy these needs?
- What is unique about these products and services?
- Who are the potential customers and where are they located?
- Why will customers select this business as their source for these products or services?
- How will these customers be reached?
- How will sales be closed?

You may struggle a little to get these two brief sections to accurately describe your business, but it's worth the struggle. The objective is not to make this task easy - but rather to make you think clearly and in some depth about the basic nature of your business. Without this clarity it is not possible to complete the balance of the planning process in an orderly and reliable way. As a small business owner, you must be as precise as possible in defining your business. It is the beginning step in allocating your limited time and resources effectively as the business evolves.

TechServ Concept Model

Let's begin to create a fictitious business to demonstrate the use of the planning models, and then later we'll see how the information from the models is used to create a complete business plan. We will start the process by entering the business concept and market opportunity information for our fictitious business on a blank Concept Model worksheet, just as you will do for your target business. This worksheet appears at the end of this chapter.

Our fictitious business will be a technology services company. As you read the brief business concept and market opportunity descriptions, think about how descriptive a few sentences can be in focusing on the fundamental nature of the business.

For example, we now know:

- It is an *information technology* business.
- It will be both a *service and a product* business.
- They will carry *quality brand-name products*.
- They have *state-of-the-art technical skills* and will maintain those skills.
- Their customers will be *small businesses*.
- They will operate in the *metropolitan area*.
- They have *experience in this type of business in this area*.
- They expect the *customer demand to increase* as the application of business technology increases.
- They expect to compete based upon *superior service, quality products* and *superior technical skills*.
- They anticipate their growth will be *gradual* and that *maintaining long-term customer relationships* will be part of their evolutionary strategy.

A complete Business Plan for TechServ has been provided in Part IV. It was developed from the information drawn from the basic planning models with some additional detail not discussed in this guide. You too will accumulate information that can be used to flesh out the basic information in your models to create your own comprehensive business plan.

Chapter Summary

Once the business concept and market opportunity have been defined on the Concept Model, the context has been established for dealing with all of the topics that follow. In effect, there is now a baseline to use as a marker to position and measure other decisions. Without such a marker, it is difficult to evaluate the impact of other business decisions. This does not mean that the definitions of the business concept and market opportunity are cast in stone. As the learning and planning for the business continues, you may find that changes in these original definitions are appropriate based upon new information. That is what is expected to happen. Making adjustments as new information becomes available is how businesses survive and grow.

Your Task

It is time now for you to complete the business concept and market opportunity parts of the blank Concept Model in Appendix A. I suggest you do it in pencil so that changes can be made easily. Don't worry about the quality of your writing. <u>Do</u> pay attention to the logic and accuracy of your content.

Starting a Small Business

TechServ Concept Model

1. Ownership and Identification --
A. Legal Form:
B. Owner's Name
C. Business Name:
D. Business Address:
E. Website Name (URL):

2. Business Concept (5 sentences) --
Our business concept is to create a full-service information technology business to meet the technical support needs of customers in the metropolitan area. We will provide both services and products to the small to mid-sized business marketplace. We will maintain, repair or replace hardware and software common to small businesses. We will carry quality brand name products that will enhance our image as a top-of-the-line provider. We will maintain state-of-the-art technical skills and equipment.

3. Market Opportunity (5 sentences) --
Having been in this industry as an employee of a similar business for several years, I can see a growing need for these products and services as the use of technology expands in the small business community. Most small business people are ill equipped to handle their own information technology needs when they have breakdowns or need upgrades and additions. They are not comfortable asking large, expensive technology service companies for assistance. Superior service coupled with quality products and good customer service at a fair price will establish a strong customer base over time.

4. Goals (3) --
A.

B.

C.

5. Strategies (one or more per goal) ---

A.

B.

C.

Legal Form and Other Legal Issues	2

Introduction

By this point you have developed a preliminary description of the business concept and market opportunity for your target business. This provides a baseline for making decisions about the legal issues that arise as you continue to define and develop your business.

In this chapter, we will consider the following business issues, all of which have some legal implication:

- Legal form - how your business is viewed from a legal and tax perspective.
- Selecting and registering a business name.
- Reserving a website domain name.
- State, county and city licenses and permits.
- Zoning, covenants and other local restrictions on business location.
- Contracts and warranties.
- Types of insurance.
- Understanding the value of an exit strategy.

Although these legal issues may sound intimidating, they can be addressed in a fairly orderly and straightforward manner. More specialized businesses may need to address more specialized issues. For example, if there is a need for a patent or trademark, specialized legal guidance may be warranted. Keep in mind that the goal in this chapter is to provide basic background information. It may be prudent for you to retain the services of an attorney or accountant as you set up your own business.

Legal Form

Legal form or structure refers to how your business is viewed from a legal and a tax perspective. It is important that you understand the characteristics of the common legal forms sufficiently to make an informed decision. The differences are relatively easy to understand.

Starting a Small Business

There are five legal structures commonly used by small businesses:

1. Sole Proprietor
2. Partnership
3. Limited Liability Company (LLC)
4. "C' Corporation
5. "S" Corporation

The decision of which legal form to select usually depends upon the answers to the following questions:

1. Do you want to have maximum liability protection of your personal assets? *yes*.
2. Is there now, or might there be in the future, more than one owner? *yes*
3. Is there the possibility of selling the business in the future? *no*.

If the answer to any one of these questions is "yes", then you should seriously consider a Limited Liability Company (LLC) or an "S" Corporation. Both of these legal entities will provide the structure to accommodate all three of these conditions, and they provide good tax treatment. As you review the following information on legal form, keep your thoughts on these three questions in mind.

We will discuss the following aspects of each structure:

- Requirements to establish the legal form.
- General tax treatment.
- Protection of personal assets from business liability claims.

Other issues may be important in specific business situations, but these are the three issues that concern most new small business startups.

Sole Proprietor

Establishing a sole proprietorship is the simplest of all the legal forms. You are in business by saying you are in business and you can terminate the business in the same fashion. This does not mean that you don't have liabilities that continue beyond the termination of the business. Let's consider the three issues listed above.

Requirements:
You may need to register your business name, get permits or licenses, and check zoning and location restrictions, depending upon the nature of your business. We will discuss these items later in this chapter.

Starting a Small Business

Tax Treatment:
The tax treatment for a sole proprietor is the same as if you were employed by any other organization. Earnings are posted to your social security number, and taxed as personal income. Usually this is as good a tax rate as you can get.

Legal Liability:
The most important issue for a sole proprietor is potential liability. As a sole proprietor, there is no separation between your personal assets and your business assets. As a result, your personal assets may be subject to a business liability claim. If there is even a remote possibility that practicing your business could result in a liability claim, then you may want to consider a different legal form and/or secure some insurance protection.

Partnership

Requirements:
Establishing a partnership merely requires an agreement between two or more people. Other issues, such as business name and licenses and permits, are the same as for the sole proprietorship.

Tax Treatment:
The tax treatment for the partners is the same as for the sole proprietorship. Each partner pays tax based upon his income from the business.

Legal Liability:
The issue of liability is very significant in a partnership because each partner may be held responsible for business commitments or liability claims resulting from actions of the other partner. This makes a partnership a potentially dangerous legal form and warrants special attention.

If a partnership structure is selected, it is important to create a written agreement that spells out all of the details of the arrangement, including such things as financial contributions, roles and responsibilities, allocation of income, salaries and benefits, and how to alter or end the relationship.

Limited Liability Company (LLC)

This is a relatively new legal structure and is becoming quite popular because of its simplicity and liability protection. You will want to check out the regulations for establishing an LLC in your state, but the following general rules apply in most states.

Starting a Small Business

Requirements:
Establishing a Limited Liability Company is accomplished by completing a simple form obtained from the state agency that authorizes and maintains business records. Forms are usually available on the agency website. There is usually a small fee of $50.00 to $100.00 for registering the business.

Tax Treatment:
If the LLC is going to be owned by one person, it is treated like a sole proprietorship from a tax perspective. If there are multiple owners, then it is treated like a partnership from a tax perspective.

Legal Liability:
One of the advantages of an LLC is that it is a legal entity. Therefore, the personal assets of the owners are not subject to business liability claims.

If there are multiple owners, it is important to create a written agreement that spells out the details of the arrangement. This should include ownership allocation, financial contributions, roles and responsibilities, operational and other policy statements, transfer or sale of ownership rights, and adding owners.

"C" Corporation

Requirements:
Establishing a "C" Corporation is accomplished by completing a simple form obtained from the state agency that authorizes and maintains business records. This form is called the "Articles of Incorporation". Forms are usually available on the agency website. There is usually a fee of $50.00 to $100.00 for registering the corporation. A corporation provides for shares of stock to represent ownership rights. Stock can be sold and additional stock issued to bring in additional owners and capital. When a corporation is initially registered, it is identified as a "C" corporation.

Tax Treatment:
At this point in time, corporate earnings and distributed dividends are taxed, resulting in double taxation. This issue is under review by Congress as this book goes to press.

Legal Liability:
One of the advantages of a corporation is that it is a legal entity and the personal assets of the owners are not subject to business liability claims.

Corporations provide for organizational structure and policies through by-laws and other legal agreements that spell out roles and responsibilities of the Board of Directors and corporate officer positions. However, one individual can completely own and control a corporation and fill all of the officer positions.

"S" Corporation

Requirements:
A sub-chapter "S" corporation is established by forming a "C" corporation (as outlined above) and then filing a form with the Internal Revenue Service to change to "S" status.

Tax Treatment:
There are some other considerations that may be relevant and you may want to discuss these matters with an attorney or a tax consultant to be sure of their impact on your business. For example, as the president of a "C" corporation, you may be able to pay for certain benefits, such as health insurance, as a company expense because you are an employee of the company. You may not be able to do this as the president of an "S" corporation.

Legal Liability:
An "S" corporation perpetuates the liability protection of the corporation but gives the owners tax treatment like an individual.

Other Legal Issues

There are a number of other legal issues that may be important in forming your business. Consider each of the following topics and determine how they may impact your business.

Selecting and Registering a Business Name

If you are going to operate the business as a sole proprietor or partnership, and you want to operate under a name different from your legal name, you should consider registering the business name with the state. If you do, this will be identified as a trade name. Registering the name will ensure that the name is not already in use by someone who may decide to take legal action against you. It will provide you the same protection in the future.

Starting a Small Business

If you form an LLC or a corporation, part of the registration process is a check against existing business names in the state to make sure you are not duplicating one.

You should also consider the advertising value of the name you select. For a small business, it is often beneficial if the business name suggests the nature of the business. If you follow this approach, every business card or other form of written advertising tells potential customers about your business.

Finally, if you think that you might want to sell your business at a future date, it is easier if the business name is "transparent". "Transparent" means that the business could change hands without the public or your customers being aware that a change had taken place. A new owner could easily assume the responsibility for the existing business. If the business is under your legal name, transparency is lost.

Reserving a Website Name

These days it is routine for businesses (even small ones) to have websites. As a result of the popularity of the Web, many new business names have already been adopted for websites (URLs). If you think you may want a website, it is prudent to select a matching website name and business name before you register the business name with the state.

Licenses, Permits, Zoning and Covenants

There are basically two issues that emerge from this section. First, it is critical to obtain the appropriate work licenses or permits for yourself and your employees. Secondly, it is necessary to determine whether it is legal for the business to be conducted at the location selected.

Most states require that individuals or businesses performing certain types of work have state certificates or licenses. Examples include professionals such as doctors, certified public accountants, and architects. State licenses are often required for construction and home repair businesses. People in these professions need to understand state and federal licensing requirements. Many other small businesses, such as consulting firms don't require a license. It is important to check with the county clerk and make sure that no license is required.

The second concern is business location. Many small businesses can be operated out of a residence and don't require approval. Your county clerk can confirm the regulations in your area. However, a community or sub-division may have covenants of its own that restrict certain types of business activity, so it is best to contact your association president for approval of a home-based business.

If you are going to buy or lease property as a business location, you need to be sure that the location is zoned for your type of business. Again, the county clerk can determine if the zoning matches your business classification.

Government regulations indicate that if you are planning to have employees or if you establish a corporation or a Limited Liability Company, you probably need to get a Federal Employer Identification Number (EIN). This number is secured by completing and submitting an IRS form that can be obtained online or by calling the IRS. The state also requires that a retail business that sells products have a sales tax license so that sales tax can be collected and paid to the state treasury.

Contracts and Warranties

If your business concept involves providing estimates, written contracts or warranties that you are responsible for supporting, it is recommended that you have an attorney develop these documents for you, or at least review the documents you plan to use. Such documents represent legal commitments that you must honor, so they need to be drafted in a manner that limits your liability.

Insurance Protection

As a business owner, you should consider the need for business insurance, just as you do for various types of personal protection (health, property damage, etc.). There is insurance available for almost any purpose. Insurance for liability and the protection of assets from fire, water, wind and theft are the most common. Start with your present insurer and obtain recommendations based upon your business model. Even if you have selected a legal form that protects your personal assets from business liability claims, you will still need some form of business insurance to protect business assets.

Planning for an Exit Strategy

"Exit strategy" is the term used to describe the conditions under which an owner expects to leave the business. It may seem strange to bring this topic up at the time the business is being formed, but if you are forming a business with multiple owners, the conditions under which an owner leaves the business should be defined as part of the startup agreement. At a minimum, the agreement should spell out the rights of departing owners and how they will be compensated for their contributions to the business. It is almost impossible to reach an amicable agreement on these issues after the business has existed for a period of time. This principle applies to any multi-owner business, regardless of its legal form.

TechServ Concept Model

The information covered in this chapter is very important in establishing a new business, and the decisions made are critical to its future. However, they don't require complex entries on the Concept Model. In the case of our fictitious business, the following decisions were made:

- Even though it is a one-owner business now, we decided that it should be a Limited Liability Company to protect personal assets and facilitate a possible future sale. This also makes it easier for the owner to add his wife as an owner at any time. In fact, TechServ could become a "woman-owned business" if that were beneficial, by making his wife the majority owner.
- The business name selected was "TechServ". This name provides transparency, suggests the nature of the business, and is currently available.
- This same name was available as a website name. If we decide to proceed with the business, we will reserve it for future use.
- We decided to start as a home-based business and move into a leased space as soon as we have some income stability from established customers.

The appropriate additions were made to the TechServ Concept Model.

Chapter Summary

Let's summarize some of the key points made in this chapter:

- There are three important questions that guide your choice of a legal entity (liability issues, multiple ownership, and sale of the business).
- Select a legal form that meets your requirements. Don't be scared off by the formality of establishing a corporation or Limited Liability Company!
- If you have now, or expect to have in the future, a multi-owner business, draft a specific written agreement between the owners.
- Obtain a business name and a website domain name concurrently.
- Research the need for and secure any licenses, permits and zoning or covenant approvals.
- Confirm any insurance requirements.
- Consider the need for an exit agreement.

Your Task

Your task is to perform the research required to make the decisions outlined above for your business. Keep a record of the assumptions you used to reach these decisions for inclusion in your business plan. Make the appropriate entries on your Concept Model.

Starting a Small Business

TechServ Concept Model

1. Ownership and Identification --

A. Legal Form: Limited Liability Company (LLC)

B. Owner's Name: Robert T. Bodine

C. Business Name: TechServ, LLC

D. Business Address: 1244 Milton Street, Columbia, MD 21055

E. Website Name (URL): TechServ.com

2. Business Concept (5 sentences) --

Our business concept is to create a full-service information technology business to meet the technical support needs of customers in the metropolitan area. We will provide both services and products to the small to mid-sized business marketplace. We will maintain, repair or replace hardware and software common to small businesses. We will carry quality brand name products that will enhance our image as a top-of-the-line provider. We will maintain state-of-the-art technical skills and equipment.

3. Market Opportunity (5 sentences) --

Having been in this industry as an employee of a similar business for several years, I can see a growing need for these products and services as the use of technology expands in the small business community. Most small business people are ill equipped to handle their own information technology needs when they have breakdowns or need upgrades and additions. They are not comfortable asking large, expensive technology service companies for assistance. Superior service coupled with quality products and good customer service at a fair price will establish a strong customer base over time.

4. Goals (3) ---

A.

B.

C.

5. Strategies (one or more per goal) --

A.

B.

C.

D.

The Task Plan	3

Introduction

We are far enough along in the learning and planning process to introduce and begin to use the Task Plan. The Task Plan is a version of a PERT chart (Program Evaluation and Review Technique). The Task Plan is used to itemize the significant tasks to be completed and indicates target dates for completion. If tasks have a sequential relationship, it is indicated by the order and timing of the schedule. This planning tool is being introduced now because we have been discussing different tasks required to implement the business and we want to keep track of them as they surface. A blank copy of the Task Plan is included in Appendix A. You can also review the Task Plan for TechServ at the end of this chapter.

Three Planning Stages

The Task Plan is divided into three sections, assuming that the business has not been started as yet. If the business is already underway, then the first two stages are not required. The three stages are:

- Planning and Evaluation
- Pre-Startup
- Post-Startup

These are not difficult concepts and we won't make them any more difficult than they are. However, you should not discount the value of this tool because of its simplicity. As we will discuss in the next chapter, it is important to set planning goals that are specific and have completion dates. The Task Plan is your vehicle to address both of these issues.

The format of the Task Plan is very simple. Significant tasks are listed in the left column; the time frame for completion is indicated in the monthly (or weekly) columns with a dotted line. The dotted line can be changed to a solid line when the task is completed. Tasks should be placed in sequential order based upon their starting dates.

Starting a Small Business

Planning and Evaluation Stage

The Planning and Evaluation Stage covers the period you are in right now as you learn about business and begin to define your own business. By the end of this stage you should be able to decide if it makes sense to proceed with implementation of the business. You may be researching a number of different topics at any point in time during this stage. It is best if you list only major tasks on the Task Plan to keep your status as clear as possible. You will also be identifying tasks that will need to be performed during the other two stages, assuming that the business decision is "to proceed". Make entries in the other stages of the Task Plan as these issues arise so that you don't lose the thought. You will probably have to revise the content and order of the Task Plan as more tasks are identified. Some tasks will turn out to be dependent upon the completion of other tasks and these relationships will trigger revisions in order and timing.

Pre-Startup Stage

The Pre-Startup Stage starts after the Planning and Evaluation Stage has been completed and the decision has been made to proceed with the business initiative. This is the period where the major tasks required to actually start doing business are identified. This is not to say that everything must be in place because some tasks may require an extended period of time to complete. But at least the essentials are in place in order to begin to make sales and meet customer commitments.

Focus on priorities! Your highest priority in the pre-startup stage is to make sure that you have met legal requirements that govern your relationship with regulatory agencies, suppliers or customers. It may not matter if your product inventory isn't quite complete or some of your advertising media is still being developed as long as you can satisfy customer requests. Once the "die is cast", it is important to start generating income as quickly as possible. The Task Plan is an excellent vehicle for identifying those "critical path" items that will permit you to open your doors for business.

Post-Startup Stage

The Post-Startup Stage of the Task Plan identifies those items that require attention during the period immediately after opening your doors for business. It is best if the Task Plan covers at least the first twelve months after starting the business. The reasons for this will become more obvious when we get to the chapter on the Financial Model. It boils down to anticipating tasks that may result in the need for allocation of financial resources. It is important to program all of the major expenses into the Financial Model. Tasks that will require an expenditure of money or time need to be identified and scheduled as part of the Planning and Evaluation Stage.

TechServ Task Plan

We have started a Task Plan for TechServ to demonstrate its usefulness. We will update it as we identify tasks to be performed. We have entered the following items in the Planning and Evaluation Stage and allocated one month for each:

- Complete the planning tasks outlined in this book.
- Evaluate the business opportunity and make a decision about proceeding.
- Prepare a complete business plan to provide the additional details of the business.

We also began to insert some tasks to be completed during the Pre-Startup Stage, if we do decide to proceed with the initiative:

- Form the Limited Liability Company.
- Reserve a website name.
- Get rental estimates on possible leased space locations.
- Get an insurance quote for home-based and leased space.

Chapter Summary

It is important to understand and accept the idea that things do not get done without a plan. Anticipate things that need to be done, develop a schedule to ensure they are done at the appropriate time, and measure their impact on human and financial resources.

Your Task

Start to make entries on the Task Plan for your business.

Starting a Small Business

TechServ Task Plan						
A. Planning and Evaluation Stage	**1**	**2**	**3**			
1. Complete tasks in guide 2. Perform evaluation of idea 3. Complete the business plan 4. 5. 6.	··········	··········	··········			
B. Pre-Startup Stage	**4**	**5**	**6**			
1. Form an LLC 2. Reserve website name 3. Check commercial space rates 4. Get insurance quotes 5. 6. 7. 8. 9. 10. 11. 12.	·········· ·········· ·········· ··········					
C. Post-Startup Stage	**7-8**	**9-10**	**11-12**	**13-14**	**15-16**	**17-18**
1. . 2. 3. 4. 5. 6.						

| Goals and Strategies | 4 |

Introduction

In this chapter, you will continue developing the outline of your target business. These basic business parameters provide the planning boundaries and goal posts for the more detailed activities that follow. Developing Goals and Strategies and documenting them on the Concept Model continues this process.

Visualizing images such as making big sales or depositing piles of money is easy and often accompanies the dream of a successful business. Translating those images into meaningful goals with real strategies to achieve them is not so easy. It requires all of the energy and creativity of the entrepreneur to convert these dreams into the reality of a successful competitive business.

Goals are Important

No one would start a perilous trip to a strange and unknown location without first investigating how to get there and identifying some milestones to indicate you are on the right path. That's the purpose of setting goals and developing strategies. You are developing the road map and identifying the waypoints that confirm you are on the right path.

One business-planning yardstick that might be useful to you is "what kind of information would a banker require before making a business loan to a startup business?" The topics we have covered already and the topics we will cover in future chapters address issues that concern bankers. Clearly stated goals and strategies are indicators that the owner has given thoughtful consideration to what he or she wants the business to achieve and how it will be achieved.

Goals and Strategies - 'Whats?" and "Hows?"

Most people don't set written goals with implementation strategies as part of their jobs. The terms may be strange, but they aren't strange in actual experience. First, goals and strategies go hand-in-hand. For every goal there must be one or more strategies. Second, if you convert these two words into "Whats?" and "Hows?" they immediately make sense. Goals are "what" you want to achieve, strategies are "how" you expect to achieve them. So if you aren't comfortable with the terms "goals" and "strategies", just think in terms of what you want to achieve and how you are going to achieve it. It is easy to mix goals and strategies in the same statement, but it is a mistake. Make every effort to keep the two items separate so that you can make changes to either one easily.

Mission Statement

Occasionally the question arises of whether a Mission or Vision Statement is needed. Both reflect the long-term goals of the organization. They often become the guiding principles for the business. If such statements can be used to clarify and focus attention on attaining the important internal and external goals of the business, then they serve a useful function for both employees and the public.

The following graphic depicts the relationship of the Mission Statement to the Goals and Strategies. It shows the separation of the "whats" and the "hows".

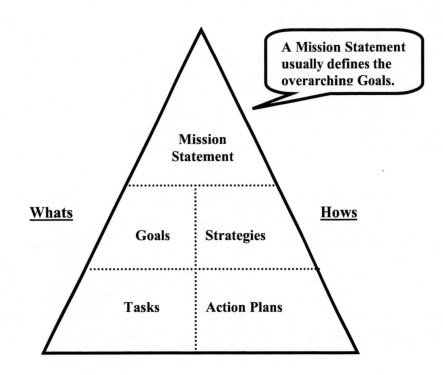

Starting a Small Business

Setting Preliminary Goals

The concept of setting business goals is so foreign to some startup entrepreneurs that they ask me what I think their goals should be. Of course, I can't presume to know what their goals should be, but I usually try to generate some conversation along the following lines. I just ask them to tell me why they want to start their own business. They respond as follows:

- I want to be able to control the source of my income.
- I want to have something I own.
- I want to have a family business.
- I want to profit from my work rather than have others profit from it.
- I want to make a fortune.
- I want to make a fortune and then sell out and do whatever I want to do.
- I can do the work better than others do it.
- I think the customers deserve something better.
- I want to treat my employees better than I am being treated.
- I want to help people and I can do a better job with my own business.
- I feel good when I do things right.
- I have an idea that is unique and I want to capitalize on it.
- I want to help protect the environment.

If you reduce these comments to their lowest common denominators you will see that they include such things as financial goals, family goals, quality of service goals, humanitarian goals, environmental goals, relationship goals and creativity goals. Some of these are business goals and some might be classified as personal goals. However, the entrepreneur expects the business environment to enable all of them to be realized. Since most owners have more than one reason for establishing their own businesses, I suggest to them that if these are reasons for going into business, then these reasons may be among their goals. If so, they need to convert them into "what" statements. This is the easy part. Let's consider the required "how" statements.

Developing Supporting Strategies

Strategies represent *actions* that will be taken to turn the goals into reality. Remember, goals are just wish lists until strategies turn them into reality. There aren't any simple secrets to developing strategies that work. Another reality is that strategies don't always produce the desired results. That doesn't mean that you give up the goal. It does mean that you have to rethink how to attain the goal and try a different strategy.

Sometimes one goal conflicts with another goal. These conflicts usually surface when you are trying to develop strategies. There could a conflict between resource allocation, timing, or some other impact on operational activities. If such a conflict occurs, you have to revisit both the goals and strategies to see what changes can be made to minimize the negative impacts of the conflict.

Let's consider two financial goals for the same company - one, a short-term goal and the other a long-term goal. The short-term goal is to reach a break-even point (income equals expenses) within the first year and a long-term goal is to reach 20 % profitability (income after expenses) by the second year and beyond. The strategy for the first year might be to take any business that comes through the door (even though it isn't very profitable) just to pay the expenses and overhead. The strategy for the long-term goal may be to develop a base of repeat customers that can generate a higher level of profitability. It may take an entirely different marketing strategy to gain access to and establish relationships with more profitable customers.

Finally, if you can't define a single, practical strategy to achieve a particular goal, then you may need to modify or drop the goal. To be of value, a goal must have a reasonable possibility of attainment and this is determined by the effectiveness of the associated strategy. If the goal cannot be attained, it may turn into a frustration that ultimately may have a negative impact on the business. The rule is to establish goals that don't set the bar so high you are doomed to failure.

TechServ Concept Model

We have entered three goals and related strategies on the Concept Model for TechServ:

- The first goal is financial.
- The second goal is to create a base of repeat customers.
- The third goal is to establish a reputation for quality, honesty and fair treatment.

We have developed strategies for each of these goals. Some of the strategies require multi-step, sequential actions.

Chapter Summary

Let's summarize some of the key points made in this chapter:

- You need goals to establish the horizon and measure the success of the business as it progresses.
- Goals serve as milestones on your startup road map.
- Goals are only "wish lists" until they are converted into reality through strategies.
- Strategies are the action plans that will lead to attainment of the goals.
- Goals may imply conflicting strategies that have to be adjusted and balanced.

Your Task

Take a few minutes and reread the information entered on the Concept Model for TechServ. Notice how one page of information can provide a very comprehensive overview of the proposed business.

Enter your goals and strategies on your Concept Model. Double-check the goals and strategies to make sure there are no unintended conflicts. Verify that the complete context of information and decisions blend together into an accurate and workable description of your business idea.

Add entries to your Task Plan.

Starting a Small Business

TechServ Concept Model

1. Ownership and Identification --
A. Legal Form: Limited Liability Company (LLC)
B. Owner's Name: Robert T. Bodine
C. Business Name: TechServ, LLC
D. Business Address: 1244 Milton Street, Columbia, MD 21055
E. Website Name (URL): TechServ.com

2. Business Concept (5 sentences) --
Our business concept is to create a full-service information technology business to meet the technical support needs of customers in the metropolitan area. We will provide both services and products to the small to mid-sized business marketplace. We will maintain, repair or replace hardware and software common to small businesses. We will carry quality brand name products that will enhance our image as a top-of-the-line provider. We will maintain state-of-the-art technical skills and equipment.

3. Market Opportunity (5 sentences) --
Having been in this industry as an employee of a similar business for several years, I can see a growing need for these products and services as the use of technology expands in the small business community. Most small business people are ill equipped to handle their own information technology needs when they have breakdowns or need upgrades and additions. They are not comfortable asking large, expensive technology service companies for assistance. Superior service coupled with quality products and good customer service at a fair price will establish a strong customer base over time.

4. Goals (3) --
A. Become profitable (income exceeds expense) within 12 months.
B. Build a small pool of customers that provide recurring revenues through service contracts or periodic maintenance agreements.
C. Develop a reputation for quality, honesty and fair treatment in all relationships, whether it is with customers, suppliers or employees.

5. Strategies (one or more per goal) --
A. Use the financial Model as the budget and control expenses closely.
   Quickly implement a marketing plan to reach business people I know.
   Get low-cost marketing media for distribution on a cold-calling basis.
   Negotiate the best prices from suppliers.
B. Identify 100 potential customers meeting our ideal customer profile.
   Develop an attractively priced maintenance contract.
   Offer special maintenance contract incentives during the first two years.
C. Establish a quality assurance procedure to follow up on all customer service visits.
   Clear up any outstanding issues. Always ask for referrals from current customers.

Part II:

Business Niche

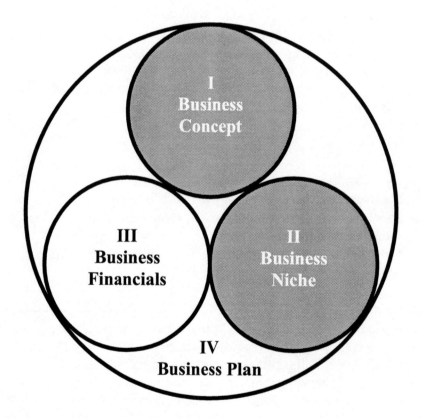

Building the Niche Model

Introduction

Chapters 5 through 8 are devoted to discussing the fundamental business elements that establish the "niche" for any business. The five elements of the Niche Model build upon the information and decisions contained in the Concept Model. The Concept Model started with brief business concept and market opportunity descriptions that began to establish the parameters of the business. The Niche Model will help us to drive these broad definitions down another level of detail.

The elements within the Niche Model are the heart of the business, and if the heart is weak or out of "sync", the business may falter. This is the time and place to perform the analysis required to confirm that the business idea is sound, providing confidence in a "go-ahead" final decision. A blank copy of the Niche Model in included in Appendix A for your use. We will create a Niche Model for TechServ as we proceed through these four chapters.

Positioning Your Business

No business provides all of the products and services needed by any one consumer, let alone all consumers. As you think about the millions of products and services that are available in the market, one business can provide only a very small portion. If we carry this obvious conclusion further, even the very largest businesses provide only a minute portion of these products and services. For example, as large as it may be, no single auto manufacturer is able to garner even 10 % of the market. They simply don't have the resources, ideas or expertise to lock up the marketplace. They cannot supply everything for everyone. Even auto manufacturers must be extremely careful in defining their segment of the market and in allocating resources to capture their portion of that market. Large businesses fail when they overextend and lose focus on their core business competencies.

Starting a Small Business

This same philosophy applies in the small business environment and is perhaps the most critical of all business decisions. To lose focus on the product/service and customer combinations that provide the greatest sales opportunities will lead to ineffective use of the very limited resources available to a small business. *The Niche Model is designed to force thoughtful consideration of the core elements that are the basis for your business.*

What is a Business Niche?

We use the following definition for a business niche. "A business niche is the composite of the business elements that define your segment in the marketplace". The Niche Model is composed of the following five elements:

- Products and Services
- Customers
- Pricing Policy
- Competitive Edge
- Promotion, Advertising and Sales.

You will notice that this definition does not include all of the elements of your business. For example, it doesn't refer to your legal form, name, insurance, or organization. These are supporting operational elements, but they don't define the core business in detail. A business must balance and integrate these five elements to be successful. The other elements of the business structure cannot compensate for lack of coherence within this five-element group. The Concept Model touched on these elements, but now these elements are defined individually and tested in combination. If there is not enough strength and synergy in this combination, then you need to identify the discrepancies and work to eliminate them. Do not assume that a miracle will take place after you are in business to wipe out the discrepancies.

Using the Niche Model

The Niche Model, like the Concept Model, concentrates its elements on one page to facilitate their analysis as individual parts and as a whole. The requirement that these elements produce a balanced and complete "whole" is central to the analytical process. Individually, the description of each element might seem to be strong and supportive of the business concept. However, if each element doesn't bring strength and legitimacy to the other elements, the premise of the core business may be weakened.

Starting a Small Business

Defining Your Products and Services

Let's start with a simple definition of products and services. Products are "hard or physical items", while services are defined as "work performed for clients". Sometimes products are the result of performing a service. For example, a lawyer in the process of consulting with a client may produce a will. The will is a hard product. A consultant may produce a business plan. It is important for the business owner to understand how clients perceive the business. Is it perceived to be a service business or a product business? This perception will play an important role in identifying the competitive edge and selecting the most effective advertising focus.

The upper left portion of the Niche Model is devoted to the description of products and services that will be offered. There is limited space so descriptions must focus on the fundamental characteristics of the products and services. Because the next chapter deals with specific customers who will utilize these products and services, fuzziness in product/service descriptions will be compounded by fuzziness in customer profiles if you are not careful. Be very specific! If you plan to offer a number of products and services, you may decide to group them in product and service categories, instead of listing individual products and services.

If you have the opportunity to offer a wide range of products or services, now is the time for you to begin to separate the "wheat from the chaff". It might appear that the more products and services you can offer, the more opportunities you have to make sales. <u>It could well be that the reverse will happen.</u> Providing too many products or services may reduce your ability to focus on your best opportunities. These decisions relate directly to creating a balanced core business in the early stages. As your business grows and resources increase, there will be time to add offerings. This is the time to focus on your strengths.

Supplier Arrangements and Inventory

If your business involves providing commercially available products, there are a number of things to consider. The first is to make sure that you have a strong supplier arrangement and more than one source for all critical products. Identifying all of your products and their sources is an important early step in confirming the validity of the Niche Model.

In the process of developing these supplier arrangements, develop your preliminary pricing approach. Identify your purchase price and your proposed selling price. The difference is your markup. These issues will be covered in more detail in Chapters 9 through 11.

This leads to the decisions regarding inventory. What are you going to keep in stock? What will you purchase after receiving a customer order? These decisions may hinge on sales and financial projections. More on this later as part of building the Financial Model.

TechServ Niche Model

We have started to create the Niche Model for TechServ. This business will offer both products and services. The sense of the owner is that it will be perceived more as a service business than a product business. The reason is that fixing problems and helping with upgrades is more service related than product related. The goal to establish a strong customer base emphasizing repeat business is built around this heavily maintenance-oriented philosophy.

TechServ Task Plan

We added "develop multiple supplier sources" to the Pre-Startup phase of the Task Plan.

Chapter Summary

Let's summarize some of the key points made in this chapter:

- The Niche Model uses five business elements to define the core business in detail. The evaluation of these five elements individually and as part of a "whole" will validate the viability of the business concept.
- Selecting the specific products and services to be offered is the first step in building the Niche Model. Controlling the variety of the offerings is an important consideration.
- It is necessary to understand the customer perception of the business as a product or service business.

Your Task

Start building your Niche Model by defining your products and services.

Add entries to your Task Plan.

TechServ Niche Model

1. **Product and Service Offerings** --
   A. Products
   - Small business software
   - Computers
   - Peripherals
   - Office networking products

   B. Services
   - Software upgrades
   - Hardware upgrades
   - Network installation and maintenance
   - On site customer training
   - Maintenance service contracts

2. **Customer Profile Characteristics** ---
   -
   -
   -
   -
   -
   -

3. **Pricing Policy Characteristics** ---
   -
   -
   -
   -
   -

4. **Competitive Edge Characteristics** ---
   -
   -
   -
   -

5. **Promotion and Advertising** ---
   -
   -
   -

Starting a Small Business

TechServ Task Plan						
A. Planning and Evaluation Stage	**1**	**2**	**3**			
1. Complete tasks in guide	••••••••					
2. Perform evaluation of idea		••••••••				
3. Complete the business plan			••••••••			
4.						
5.						
6.						
B. Pre-Startup Stage	**4**	**5**	**6**			
1. Form an LLC	••••••••					
2. Reserve website name	••••••••					
3. Check commercial space rates	••••••••					
4. Get insurance quotes	••••••••					
5. Order business telephone		••••••••				
6. Develop multiple supplier sources		••••••••				
7.						
8.						
9.						
10.						
11.						
12.						
C. Post-Startup Stage	**7-8**	**9-10**	**11-12**	**13-14**	**15-16**	**17-18**
1.						
2.						
3.						
4.						
5.						
6.						

Profiling Customers	6

Introduction

In this chapter, we will begin to identify the characteristics of the customers most likely to purchase the products and services of your business. First, let's back up a step and talk about customer needs.

The success of all businesses is based upon satisfying a customer need or want. You might view a "need" as something essential, and a "want" as a desire for something that is not a necessity. The difference between these two ideas is really just the customer perception. One customer's need is another customer's want. However, there may a difference from a business perspective because, if the customer becomes selective or if financial resources are limited, only needed products or services may be purchased.

What is the point of this discussion? It is that any potential startup business should understand very clearly which customers <u>need</u> their products or services. The success of the business will depend upon finding those customers and convincing them that you should be their supplier. If you anticipate too many sales in the "want" category, your revenue estimates may be overstated and your business concept may be severely weakened. You must be able to identify those high sales probability customers and be able to reach them effectively.

Needs Define Your Customers

The best way to start a business is to identify unmet or unsatisfied customer needs that fall under the umbrella of your business concept. Needs should come first, followed by an idea of how to reach those customers and satisfy the "needs". Sometimes an entrepreneur will select products or services without completely <u>understanding the need.</u> Forcing products and services into a niche that doesn't fit makes business success difficult.

How do you determine where there is an unmet need? There is no surefire method of making this determination at the local, small business level. New fast food restaurants always seem to be successful in reaching customers. These franchises have developed some very sophisticated methods of analyzing the demographics of an area and making accurate projections based upon this research. They have also established a reputation for a menu that has a proven demand (need or want). The typical small business doesn't have the resources to undertake such a sophisticated analysis and they don't have marketplace clout that comes with an established reputation. You are much more dependent upon your intuition and previous experience in the industry. This is one of the reasons why the small business owner should have some experience in the industry, ideally in the local area.

Developing an Ideal Customer Profile

How do you go about defining the characteristics of your "ideal customer"? The term "ideal" is used to suggest the most likely customer candidates, as compared to anyone who "might" be a customer. At least in theory, the ideal customer will produce more sales with less effort than any more general classification.

There are some questions that can help you determine these "ideal customers". First, are they consumers (non-business) or businesses? This distinction is very important; it is easier to identify specific businesses than it is to select specific, individual consumers. Let's look at each of these groups.

Business Customers

If your customers are primarily businesses, you can start by determining the size of the business that is most likely to require your products and services <u>and</u> most likely to be comfortable dealing with you as a small business. Most small businesses deal with other small to medium-sized businesses because their needs match your ability to deliver. Large businesses may require large a volume of products or services that you simply can't supply. You should focus on business customers of a size that matches your ability to deliver, as well as their perception that you can deliver.

The next step is to determine whether there are geographical boundaries for your business. If your business is dependent upon frequent face-to-face meetings with customers, then you probably have a geographical constraint of perhaps 50 to 100 miles. If your business can be conducted over the phone or Internet, then you may not have any geographical constraints.

Now that you know your geographical constraints, you can determine which industry classifications within this area have the greatest need for your products and services. As you can see, this is a winnowing process. After identifying those industry classifications most likely to need your products or services, you can begin to develop specific lists by name, location, size, etc. Now your ideal customer profile is beginning to take shape - you can start to visualize the potential size of your marketplace and what marketing approaches might be most successful. More on this in the next chapter...

There are commercially available databases that provide listings of businesses by size, industry classification, location, number of employees, sales revenue, officers, etc. Your local library probably has some of these commercial databases available online without charge. These databases don't generally provide data on smaller businesses so they may not be very useful to you. You will have to make a decision based on your unique "ideal business" profile.

Finally, don't assume that the characteristics of customers most likely to purchase your products are the same as those who purchase your services. They are often different. If necessary, develop a different ideal customer profile for each.

Consumers

Consumers are defined as non-business customers. The approach to developing an ideal consumer profile is similar to that outlined above for business customers. There are three broad sets of characteristics that describe the consumer marketplace:

- Geographic
- Demographic
- Psychographic.

1. Geographics

Geographic factors are the first filter (screening device) used to describe consumers. Most small businesses that provide products or services to consumers operate within a radius of 50 or so miles. Beyond that distance, the drive time and costs are so great that the business can't compete with closer suppliers. In metropolitan areas there are additional issues of traffic tie-ups and other factors that can impact both service and cost. Set the geographic parameters first if they are a factor. E-businesses may not have geographic limitations.

2. Demographics

Demographics refer to the specific characteristics of the decision-makers and end-users. The common list of demographic characteristics includes age, sex, marital status, income level, ethnic background, home ownership, and education. Demographic data is available from national census studies as well as from local data collection efforts. Census information is free and is broken down to the ZIP Code level. Economic development authorities at the county level can be an excellent source of information on both business and consumer demographics. As a consumer-oriented business, knowledge of your ideal consumers -- where they are located and how to reach them -- is critical. *Book : Guide for Zip Code Demographics.*

3. Psychographics

Psychographics is the term used to identify special characteristics that relate primarily to lifestyle. There are individuals and groups that have an interest in all kinds of special activities - cars, photography, health, travel, cycling, dancing, movies are examples. If your business has a special focus, then you need to be able to find consumers with the same areas of interest. Groups usually have their own media that is available to advertisers. They may make membership lists available for a fee. All of these sources are important points of contact that help identify the size and location of the consumer marketplace.

Quality Assurance and Reputation

Successful small business owners agree that providing quality products and services is the cornerstone of their reputation, and a good reputation is their most important asset. Businesses depend upon repeat business and repeat business can only be obtained if the customer is satisfied with the quality of products or services that have been provided.

As you define these five elements of your business niche, keep the need for a strong quality assurance program uppermost in your mind. Quality won't happen consistently without an operational process that provides for continuous evaluation and follow-up.

TechServ Niche Model

Our TechServ owner identified several specific "ideal customer" profile characteristics, starting with the recognition that their customers will be businesses rather than consumers. Because of the need to deliver products and services to customer sites, a radius of 50 miles from the home base seemed reasonable. A longer trip can always be scheduled if it is worthwhile. Small to mid-sized business customers, not in the information technology industry and with a sales staff, will be highlighted.

TechServ Task Plan

We added an entry to spend some time building a quality assurance process into the daily operational procedures. We also added an entry to order the startup inventory.

Chapter Summary

Let's summarize the key points made in this chapter:

- The niche planning process starts with a clear identification of unmet needs.
- Identify the pool of customers who have these needs and can afford to meet them.
- Identifying the characteristics of ideal customers within this pool is critical to being able to reach them and make sales.
- Determine if your ideal customers are business, consumer or both.
- Analyze the pertinent characteristics of your customers (volume, geography, demographics, etc.)
- Remember that your business reputation is your most valuable long-term asset.

Your Task

Continue building your Niche Model by defining your ideal customer profile. Make sure that the profile fits both your products and services (if not, develop a profile of each).

Add entries to your Task Plan.

TechServ Niche Model

1. **Product and Service Offerings** --
   A. Products
   - Small business software
   - Computers
   - Peripherals
   - Office networking products

   B. Services
   - Software upgrades
   - Hardware upgrades
   - Network installation and maintenance
   - On site customer training
   - Maintenance service contracts

2. **Customer Profile Characteristics** ---
   - Small to medium sized businesses
   - 5 to 100 employees
   - Non information technology businesses
   - Within 50 mile radius
   - Gross revenues $250,000 +
   - Has sales staff

3. **Pricing Policy Characteristics** ---
   -
   -
   -
   -

4. **Competitive Edge Characteristics** --
   -
   -
   -
   -

5. **Promotion and Advertising** --
   A. Personal Advertising
   -
   -
   -
   -

   B. Impersonal Advertising
   -
   -
   -
   -

Starting a Small Business

TechServ Task Plan						
A. Planning and Evaluation Stage	**1**	**2**	**3**			
1. Complete tasks in guide	··········					
2. Perform evaluation of idea		··········				
3. Complete the business plan			·········			
4.						
5.						
6.						
B. Pre-Startup Stage	**4**	**5**	**6**			
1. Form an LLC	··········					
2. Reserve website name	··········					
3. Check commercial space rates	··········					
4. Get insurance quotes	··········					
5. Order business telephone		·········				
6. Develop multiple supplier sources		·········				
7. Design quality assurance program			·········			
8. Order startup inventory			·········			
9.						
10.						
11.						
12.						
C. Post-Startup Stage	**7-8**	**9-10**	**11-12**	**13-14**	**15-16**	**17-18**
1. Establish relationship with independent contractors	·········					
2. Upgrade office computers and equipment.			·········			
3. Move to commercial location				·········		
4. Lease a newer van					·········	
5.						
6.						

Competitive Edge and Marketing	7

Introduction

Here's an analogy that may help you in visualizing your business. A business can be viewed as two islands connected by a bridge. Your business can be viewed as one island and the customer can be considered the other island. The products and services are on your island, while the customers and their money reside on the other island. The challenge is for you to move your products and services to the customers' island and to move their money to your island. This is called a transaction. For this to happen, we need a bridge between these two islands. You must understand how to build this bridge, because "without a bridge there is no business". The remaining three elements of the Niche Model are the mechanisms and materials used to create and maintain this transaction bridge. Let's consider those three elements - "Pricing", "Your Competitive Edge", and "Promotion and Advertising". They appear on the lower half of the Niche Model.

Building Bridges to Customers

Continuing with the analogy above, there may already be one or more bridges connecting the customer's island with your competitor's islands. In fact, it is always true, unless you happen to be the first one in the marketplace. What are the elements that determine whether you, or your competitors, can create a better bridge? One of the first things to consider is your pricing policy. Setting a price for goods and services is usually an unsettling issue for the new entrepreneur. Everyone knows that price is an important factor in making sales and the tendency is to lower prices to the point where most or all of the profit is dissipated. You may need to set lower prices to work your way into the marketplace, but it is not a sound basis for creating a profitable long-term business.

Establishing Your Pricing Policy

You must know your competition in order to create a reasonable pricing policy!! "Pricing policy" is the term used to define the range of prices you will charge for products or services, based upon a comparison with your competition. In general, you must decide if you will be lower than, equal to, or higher than your competition for equivalent products and services. So, before you set prices, you should determine what your competition is charging. Then you will have a logical business basis for your decision. Knowing your competition helps you to define your space in the marketplace. Thoroughly researching your competition is often difficult, but it is absolutely essential before committing to a new business venture.

Defining your Competitive Edge

Competitive edge is defined as "the reason why a customer will buy from you rather than your competitors". When a new business enters the marketplace without a competitive edge, it is at its own peril. As described above, competitors already have established bridges with your target customers. Of course, it will help if those bridges are somewhat rickety! Your task is to find the elements of your own bridge that customers will find more compelling than those of the existing bridges. Those elements will be your competitive edge.

Service, quality and price are three of the most common elements of a competitive edge. It has been said that the most you can hope for is to have the advantage of two of the three items. No one can maintain an advantage in all three areas for an extended period of time. It defies most economic principles to offer the best service and the best quality at the lowest price. Over time, some compromise will be required. You can start your own competitive edge analysis with these three items and then expand it to include subtle variations.

Price is a function of the cost of delivering the quality and service that you decide to provide while meeting your profitability targets. So establishing your competitive edge may require a very detailed analysis of how you expect to balance these items. Since your reputation and long-term existence require the delivery of good quality and good service, there is not a huge margin for differentiation. "Differentiation" is the term used to define how you are able to establish an identifiable, advantageous difference between you and your competitors in the eyes of the customer. In most cases you must turn to the subtleties of each of the three key factors.

Starting a Small Business

Let's mention a few to stimulate your thinking

Variety of products or services:
Can you offer a greater variety of products or services without diminishing your ability to concentrate on essentials?

Price:
Can you offer special "first time" or "one time" reductions in price? Can you use some "loss leaders" to get your foot in the door?

Quality and training of staff:
Can you emphasize either your own qualifications or those of your staff or contractors?

Warranties:
Can you offer a better warranty than your competitors?

Service contacts:
Can you offer a better service contract than your competitors?

Location:
Can you find a way to capitalize on your location? For example, are you located on a major thoroughfare? Or do you provide free parking?

Courtesy:
Are courtesy and respect to customers a relationship asset that can be emphasized?

Hours of operation:
Are your hours of operation more flexible than those of your competitors?

Ability to respond:
Are you able to respond more quickly than your competitors?

Meeting commitments:
Are you always able to meet your customer commitments?

Customer follow-up:
Do you follow-up after work is performed to verify customer satisfaction?

There are many other variations available to you. It is your job to identify those that fit comfortably within your operational procedures and can be consistently maintained over time.

After evaluating these service, quality, and price factors, you should be able to complete the pricing and competitive edge sections of the Niche Model.

Evaluating Alternative Advertising Venues

The last of the five elements on the Niche Model is "Promotion and Advertising". Promotion and advertising are your means of attracting customers and drawing them into a relationship so that sales transactions can be consummated. Sales transactions are the ultimate measure of the success of any business, but they can only be sustained and grow over a long period of time if all five Niche Model elements have been established. There are two distinct methods of reaching customers - personal or impersonal advertising. Most businesses use both methods, but many small businesses find that one or the other works best for them. Consider first the following rules for measuring advertising results.

Measuring Advertising Results

There are two important rules when developing an advertising program for a small business:

1. You must be able to measure the results.
2. You should not commit to an extensive program until you have verified the *costs and benefits*.

The application of these rules is apparent when you contact a company to order one of their products or services and the company representative asks how you heard about them. He or she is trying to determine which of several different advertising methods is getting a customer response. This is representative of the process that you should build into your advertising program.

Impersonal Advertising

Impersonal advertising includes all of those techniques that depend upon the transmission of the advertising message by means of media other than a real live person. The typical impersonal venues available in today's marketplace include:

- Print media - newspapers, magazines
- Special distribution services that include your advertising flyer with others that go to specific geographic areas
- Radio
- Television
- Internet

The advantage of impersonal advertising is that it reaches a broad audience. The disadvantages are that it is probably not focused on your ideal customers and the impersonal nature of the advertising may not trigger a positive response. It may also be too expensive for most small start-up businesses with very limited advertising budgets. Impersonal advertising works best for larger businesses that cover a wide geographical area with more than one service location.

Personal Advertising

Personal advertising techniques include:

- Face-to-face visits
- Telephone calls
- Letters addressed to the recipient with a scheduled follow-up call
- Referrals from third parties who act as surrogate salespersons
- E-mail responses to queries

Closing Sales

This guide does not attempt to provide guidance on individual sales techniques. The importance of sales skills varies by business. If you feel you are deficient in this area, you may want to consider getting the necessary training or practice. Make sure to include a task on your Task Plan.

Marketing and a Marketing Plan

Now that we have reviewed some of the elements involved in building the bridge between the customer's island and your island, we need to address the ways in which these elements (your competitive edge) can be promoted. We will discuss two terms - marketing and marketing plans.

Marketing

Marketing is really a process - a series of steps leading to a pre-defined objective. These repeatable steps are outlined in following graphic. They rely on all five elements described in the Niche Model. As you look at this marketing model, try to see it not only as a logical series of actions required to close sales, but also as a function ensuring that business continues to flow across your bridge.

Starting a Small Business

Let's do a quick analysis of this process model. It starts with defining the products and services. This is a step we have discussed and the products and services really define our business. However, as time passes the products and services may change so the process requires periodic review for changes. Next we define the customers that are most likely to buy our products and services. Then we identify our competitive edge - those things that will encourage a customer to buy from us rather than our competitors. Once we have identified these business characteristics we are ready to design and execute a promotion/advertising program. Hopefully this leads to actual sales. From sales or failure to make sales, we learn the lessons of business reality. Learn from both successes and failures. Finally, pursue repeat business sales, they are the most productive and least expensive.

The Marketing Process

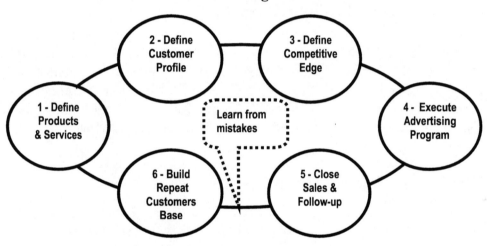

The Marketing Plan

Now, if this process seems logical, let's determine how marketing as a process relates to a marketing plan. It's very simple! Your marketing plan contains the details of how you are going to apply your marketing strategies using the steps outlined above. In other words, it's time to incorporate the details of your products and services, customer profiles, pricing and other competitive edge factors into a promotional campaign that will result in actual sales transactions. Don't forget to build in the customer follow-up to get feedback and ensure customer satisfaction.

Your goal is to create a group of loyal, repeat customers who will become the backbone of your future sales. The marketing plan should include not only the specific advertising activities that you expect to initiate, but also a periodic review of your products and services, customer profiles, pricing, sales closing techniques, etc. The marketing plan is your unique strategy for executing the marketing process for your unique business.

Making Sales Projections

One of the most challenging tasks for the new entrepreneur is making sales projections. At its best, it is not easy or reliable. At its worst, it can create a total misrepresentation of what the real world will be like. We won't be making sales projections until we create the Financial Model in Chapter 10, but the basic research for making sales projections has been completed by this stage of the planning process. As you review the decisions reflected in your Niche Model, begin to consider the actual number and type of sales you expect to make. The Financial Model will suggest that you use sales categories and average dollar amounts to form the basis for your projections. The elements of your Niche Model are transformed from descriptive representations to survival requirements.

Reviewing the Niche Model

Now let's do a quick review of the Niche Model. The Niche Model was created to add another level of detail to the conceptual view. It depicts the individual characteristics of each element as well as the close relationships between them. Information from the Niche Model will play a significant role in creating the Financial Model discussed in the next chapter.

TechServ Niche Model

We have made the following additions to the TechServ Niche Model:

- Pricing policy.
- Factors that establish our competitive edge.
- Advertising methods (both personal and impersonal will be used.)

TechServ Task Plan

We also added several items to the Task Plan for TechServ's Post-Startup Stage. We made these entries based on the assumption that the business will be opened and these tasks have financial implications that should be included in the Financial Model projections.

Chapter Summary

Let's summarize some of the key points made in this chapter:

- The need to build a strong bridge between your business and your customers.
- Other competitors have already erected their own bridges.
- The strength of your bridge will be based upon the way you define your competitive edge.
- Usually a competitive edge is based upon service, quality, and/or price. It is strengthened by more specific customer benefits that you are able to quantify and deliver.
- There are advertising venues (personal, impersonal) that promote your competitive edge to your ideal customer base most effectively.
- A marketing plan is the packaging of your unique niche elements into a logical, repeatable program.

Your Task

Your task is to complete the entries on your own Niche Model. After completing those entries, review the model for completeness and cohesiveness. Think about the adequacy of your research and decisions as a basis for making sales projections.

Make note of any areas that give you concern. You may have determined that more research is required to answer some of these questions to your own satisfaction. Has this level of detail changed your view of the viability of the business? Hopefully, it has increased your level of confidence!

Add entries to your Task Plan.

Starting a Small Business

TechServ Niche Model

1. Product and Service Offerings --
    A. Products
- Small business software
- Computers
- Peripherals
- Office networking products

    B. Services
- Software upgrades
- Hardware upgrades
- Network installation and maintenance
- On site customer training
- Maintenance service contracts

2. Customer Profile Characteristics ---
- Small to medium sized businesses
- 5 to 100 employees
- Non information technology businesses
- Within 50 mile radius
- Gross revenues $250,000 +
- Has sales staff

3. Pricing Policy Characteristics --
- Minimize providing credit - accept credit cards and checks
- Offer better prices or incentives until become established
- Products - meet or beat high volume store prices
- Services - lower than average competition in early stages

4. Competitive Edge Characteristics --
- Low prices - until well established
- Full service including system consulting
- Regular six days per week service
- Fast, friendly emergency response
- Hardware and software training
- Attractive maintenance contracts

5. Promotion and Advertising --
    A. Personal Advertising
- Visit and call known prospects
- Cold call well researched prospects
- Ask for referrals

    B. Impersonal Advertising
- Business cards and brochures
- Product advertising
- Some local inexpensive print media
- Occasional direct mail to select Zip codes

TechServ Task Plan						
A. Planning and Evaluation Stage	1	2	3			
1. Complete tasks in guide	••••••••					
2. Perform evaluation of idea		••••••••				
3. Complete the business plan			••••••••			
4.						
5.						
6.						
B. Pre-Startup Stage	4	5	6			
1. Form an LLC	••••••••					
2. Reserve website name	••••••••					
3. Check commercial space rates	••••••••					
4. Get insurance quotes	••••••••					
5. Order business telephone		••••••••				
6. Develop multiple supplier sources		••••••••				
7. Design quality assurance program			••••••••			
8. Order startup inventory			••••••••			
9. Order startup marketing media			••••••••			
10.						
11.						
12.						
C. Post-Startup Stage	7-8	9-10	11-12	13-14	15-16	17-18
1. Establish relationship with independent contractors	••••••••					
2. Upgrade office computers and equipment.			••••••••			
3. Move to commercial location				••••••••		
4. Lease a newer van					••••••••	
5.						
6.						

Management and Organization	

Introduction

As we wrap up our consideration of the Niche Model, we need to discuss one more significant issue - management and organization. There won't be any specific entries on the Niche Model for this topic, but there may be tasks that address management concerns on the Task Plan. This is a topic that warrants its own section in the business plan.

If you are starting a business with 10 or more employees, management structure and organizational issues are an extremely important aspect of your operational planning. Supervision, skill sets, job descriptions, hiring, training, personnel policies, pay scales, and employee evaluations are front-and-center issues that require a great deal of attention. You may well need the assistance of a human resources specialist who can help you with the state and federal, procedural and documentation requirements.

In the smaller business environment consisting of one or two owners and one or two employees, these issues are still important, but they require much less attention.

Nevertheless, there are two basic issues to discuss - industry knowledge and the owner's ability to handle the variety of management tasks. Let's consider these two issues.

Know Your Industry

It is common knowledge that a high number of small business startups fail. We won't try to chronicle all of the reasons, but one major reason is the owner's lack of knowledge about the industry selected. Talk to anyone familiar with counseling small business owners and they will tell you that it is extremely dangerous to start a business in which you have no personal experience. The reason is that without some actual experience in the industry, your ability to make judgments and understand the impact of decisions is severely limited.

Starting a Small Business

So, if you don't have sufficient experience in your target business, what can you do? First, you can conduct research to learn as much as possible about the business. This will help, but it may not be enough. Second, you can bring a partner or advisor into the business to supplement your knowledge and experience. It is always valuable to have an experienced mentor available to discuss issues and check judgment. Third, if circumstances permit, get a job in the industry, perhaps on a part-time basis, to gain first-hand knowledge. If your industry knowledge is limited and you are unable to supplement it with any of these options, proceed with great caution.

Wearing Many Hats

You have probably seen an organization chart for a large corporation. There are vice presidents for product/service design and development, manufacturing, distribution, marketing, sales and service, billing and collecting, human resources and training, legal, financial, benefits and payroll, and so on. Each vice president concentrates on his or her area of responsibility, becomes an expert in that field, and doesn't worry about the other areas of the business. You don't have that luxury as a small business owner. You are the one who must perform those roles in your business, or hire someone to do them for you. Realistically speaking, you probably can't afford to outsource many of them.

As a result, you have to be willing to learn enough about each of these areas to meet the demands of your business. The depth of knowledge required will vary greatly by business, but every business embodies some of these functions. As noted above, if you don't have the required experience, having regular access to a mentor is one way to identify the critical areas and get advice on how to develop the requisite skills.

Time Management

Lack of knowledge or skill in any of these important areas also affects your time management. The highest priority for a small business owner is to respond to customer needs in a timely manner. Allocating time to management functions is difficult. The more effective you are in dealing with these management functions, the more effective you become as a total business. Plan to identify and learn the things you don't know. Let the Task Plan be the initial management tool to make sure nothing falls through the cracks.

Starting a Small Business

Process and Operational Documentation

Let me explain what I mean when I use the terms *process* and *operational* documentation. The terms refer to the definition and documentation of procedures that are used in the business to consistently replicate the product of the business.

For example, a business consultant might have a process to help a client prepare a business plan or a marketing plan or a financial plan. It would be a process if it is clearly defined and is capable of being used (with some variation) with different clients in different circumstances. Having a documented process might give a potential client more confidence in the consultant. It also generally makes the consultant more efficient and organized and may result in more competitive pricing.

In another situation, the business may manufacture a hard product. In this case, the operational tasks and tools used to produce the product should be standardized and documented. This will increase the probability of producing the same quality product even if staffing or other operational changes occur.

These types of documentation are critical components of the business but are in addition to the planning process we are using in this guide. If your business concept includes either of these documentation requirements, insert the required tasks to see that they are accomplished before opening your doors for business.

Let me give you one example of operational documentation. Another consultant (really a competitor, but also a strategic partner) and I were working with a client on a strategic funding and marketing plan for an invention he developed. The invention was a wonderful idea. It would produce ice using the sun as an energy source and would work in areas of the world where no electricity was available but sunny days were the norm. Our client wanted to get funding to market the product to countries in need of such a product. They would be licensed to manufacture the invention in their country for their citizen's use. The problem was that although the device worked very well, it was just in a prototype stage and the engineering drawings needed to produce the components on a production basis were not available. We encouraged the client to develop these drawings so that potential customers could evaluate the manufacturing costs, complexities and potential profit. We were never able to convince the client to put in the effort to develop these operational documents. This may be one of the reasons that the funding and marketing plan had difficulty gaining traction. So, get your process or operational documentation tasks on your task plan.

TechServ Task Plan

We have added a task to acquire additional expertise in the form of a mentor.

Chapter Summary

This chapter emphasizes the importance of having the industry knowledge and management skills required to successfully operate the business. If you don't have the knowledge or skills, it is time to make plans to fill this critical operational gap.

Your Task

Reflect honestly on your overall knowledge and management skills and develop plans to compensate for any weaknesses you find. Decide if you have process or operational documentation requirements.

Add entries to your Task Plan.

Starting a Small Business

TechServ Task Plan						
A. Planning and Evaluation Stage	**1**	**2**	**3**			
1. Complete tasks in guide	··········					
2. Perform evaluation of idea		··········				
3. Complete the business plan			··········			
4.						
5.						
6.						
B. Pre-Startup Stage	**4**	**5**	**6**			
1. Form an LLC	··········					
2. Reserve website name	··········					
3. Check commercial space rates	··········					
4. Get insurance quotes	··········					
5. Order business telephone		··········				
6. Develop multiple supplier sources		··········				
7. Design quality assurance program			··········			
8. Order startup inventory			··········			
9. Order startup marketing media			··········			
10. Find an experienced mentor			··········			
11.						
12.						
C. Post-Startup Stage	**7-8**	**9-10**	**11-12**	**13-14**	**15-16**	**17-18**
1. Establish relationship with independent contractors	··········					
2. Upgrade office computers and equipment			··········			
3. Move to commercial location				··········		
4. Lease a newer van					··········	
5.						
6.						

Part III:
Business Financials

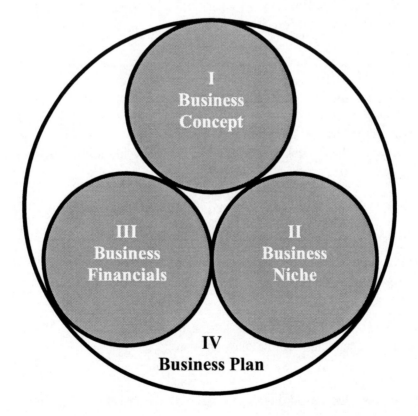

Financial Reports	9

Introduction

It is time to develop the third level of detail represented by various financial reports and projections. This is where the "rubber meets the road". Until now, the planning process may have seemed to be a purely theoretical exercise. The final step is to answer the question "how well does the concept meet the financial requirements for a successful initiative?" This is another spot where we need to reflect on "how would a banker/lender view this business from an investment perspective?" From a practical standpoint, this is how you should view the opportunity.

While counseling people who are considering startup business opportunities, often I find they have completed their financial projections without doing the kind of analysis and decision-making that is required. When I probe a little deeper about their ideas, there are often important gaps in their financial assumptions. Their original projections cannot be supported and they must replicate what we have already done to produce reliable projections.

Let's look at the financial planning requirements for a typical small business startup.

Three Key Reports

There are three financial reports that are used on a regular basis in the business and financial marketplace. They are:

1. Balance Sheet
2. Income/Expense Statement (also called a Profit and Loss Statement)
3. Cash Flow Statement

Starting a Small Business

We will review these financial reports in Chapters 9 - 11. In an existing business they represent actual business results, while in our case they are estimated projections of what we expect to happen. Our projections are identified as *pro forma* reports because they represent projections, not historical facts. There is a fourth financial projection called "Startup Expenses" that we will discuss first, followed by the Balance Sheet.

The idea of maintaining financial records, learning accounting procedures, and preparing government reports greatly distresses many new entrepreneurs. This is understandable, but like many other aspects of business, financial functions are important and require the owner's full attention. This is an area of business that lends itself to the use of outside assistance, if you desire. However, there is nothing in the financial planning area that requires more than common sense and the ability to add, subtract, multiply and divide. These are the final pieces to put your business house in order - don't neglect them.

Estimating Startup Expenses

Startup expenses are those expenses that you incur prior to opening your door for business. They vary greatly by the type of business. For example, if you are going into the consulting business and need only your knowledge, an existing computer, an existing car and a business telephone, the startup costs may not be very significant. On the other hand, if you are starting a construction business and need to buy expensive tools, equipment and some inventory items, then the startup expenses may be substantial. Our job is to figure out what is required in order for you to start your business.

The way that I begin to develop a startup expense list is by dividing the various expenses into two categories - asset-creating expenses and non-asset-creating expenses. The significance is that the asset-creating expenses are items that have inherent salvage value should the business fail, while the non-asset-creating expenses will have little or no salvage value. This distinction is important for two reasons.

First, if the business fails, the asset-creating items can be sold to pay outstanding bills or to provide some funds to the owner (probably not nearly as much as the original cost). The second reason is that bankers prefer to loan money for items with salvage value. The banker may want you to spend your own money on the non-asset-creating expenses, while he funds the purchase of asset-creating items. He may retain ownership rights to those items (as well as other business and personal assets). Recognizing the nature of your start-up expenses is an important aspect of understanding the financial basis of your business opportunity. Let's look at a list of some possible startup expense items.

Starting a Small Business

Non-Asset-Creating Expenses

1. Planning expenses
2. Legal/professional fees
3. Licenses and permits
4. Utility installations
5. Some renovations
6. Marketing media

Asset-Creating Expenses

1. Utility deposits
2. Lease deposits
3. Furniture
4. Office equipment
5. Office supplies
6. Inventory

There will be accounting and tax implications connected with all of these expenditures. Even though the non-asset-creating expenses may not have salvage value, they are legitimate expenses and can be declared as deductions against revenues from a tax perspective. The asset-creating expenditures may be classified as capital or expense items, depending upon their specific use. If you have major expenses for startup, it may be worthwhile to have an accountant advise you on techniques that can minimize your risk. The cost of this professional advice is also a deductible expense.

The startup expense list begins the process of identifying the amount of cash required to start the business. These expenses occur before the business opens and therefore cannot be paid out of sales revenues. This leads us to a discussion of the Balance Sheet.

Preparing a Balance Sheet

A Balance Sheet is a snapshot in time that reflects the assets, liabilities and net worth of an individual or a business. It is a snapshot because within moments after it is prepared the amount of assets or liabilities may have changed dramatically. For example, the value of common stock rises and falls throughout the day. Most things don't change dramatically within a short time, but some things do. That's why it is considered a snapshot. Let's define assets, liabilities and net worth.

Starting a Small Business

An Asset is something you own that has value. Assets are divided into current and fixed assets. Current assets are items like cash, checking and savings accounts. Either they are cash or can be converted into cash within one year. Fixed assets are items like real estate that may require a year or more to convert into cash.

Liabilities follow the same kind of rules. Current liabilities are obligations due now such as credit card bills, utility bills, and insurance payments. Long-term liabilities are for things like home mortgages that are due in incremental payments or not due for over a year.

Net worth is the difference between total assets and total liabilities. Net worth can be positive or negative. You may have more assets than liabilities or the reverse. Having more liabilities than assets is the main reason businesses fail or go into bankruptcy. A positive net worth is a primary indicator of collateral for a loan.

The Balance Sheet that follows has most of the common entries for a personal balance sheet. If it were for a business, there might be entries for equipment, inventory, etc. The liabilities would also be somewhat different, but the format is the same. We use this format as an example because, as a startup business, your personal assets are usually the basis for funding the startup. A banker will want to see your personal balance sheet, as well as one for your business before discussing possible loans.

Computing Startup Expenses First

The reason we completed the Startup Expenses list first is to get an idea of how much cash will be required to open the doors. Next, we complete the Balance Sheet to identify how much cash is available from personal funds.

Using the following TechServ Startup Expenses as an example, we see that they total $4350. The owner's personal balance sheet indicates that there is cash or cash equivalent available of $11,450. This indicates that there are sufficient funds available to cover startup expenses, assuming that the owner wants to commit the funds to TechServ. If additional funds are required in the Post-Startup Stage, we may not have the full funding story until later.

Starting a Small Business

Balance Sheet

A. Assets			
1. Current Assets			
Cash			
Checking Account			
Savings Account			
Bonds			
Other			
Sub-Total			
2. Fixed Assets			
Real Estate (home)			
Automobiles			
410 K			
Tools/Computers			
Furniture			
Other			
Sub-Total			
3. Total Assets			
B. Liabilities			
1. Current Liabilities			
Credit Cards			
Utilities			
Other			
Sub-Total			
2. Long Term Liabilities			
Real Estate Mortgage			
Automobiles			
Other			
Sub-Total			
3. Total Liabilities			
C. Net Worth (A.3 - B.3)			

TechServ Startup Expenses and Balance Sheets

We created a Startup Expense List, a personal Balance Sheet, and a starting Balance Sheet for TechServ. The TechServ Balance Sheet assumes the transfer of $5,000 from the owner's personal Balance Sheet to the business.

TechServ Task Plan

We did not add any entries to the Task Plan.

Chapter Summary

Let's summarize some of the key points made in this chapter:

- Four financial reports are needed to evaluate a startup business. They are: Startup Expenses, Balance Sheet, Financial Model and Cash Flow Statement. (The first two were covered in this chapter.)
- Startup expenses include asset-creating and non-asset-creating expenses.
- Personal and business balance sheets are required to fully evaluate the financial position of the business.

Your Task

Develop a Startup Expense List, a Personal Balance Sheet and a Business Balance Sheet.

Add entries to your Task Plan.

TechServ Startup Expenses

Non-Asset Creating Startup Expenses		
1. Planning Expenses	150	
2. Legal/Professional Fees	200	
3. Licenses and Permits	0	
4. Utility Installations	0	
5. Renovations	250	
6. Marketing Media	400	
7. Checking Account	100	
Total Non-Asset Startup Expenses		1100
Asset Creating Startup Expenses		
1. Utility Deposits	0	
2. Lease Deposits	0	
3. Furniture	350	
4. Office Equipment	250	
5. Office supplies	150	
6. Inventory	2000	
7. Tools	500	
Total Asset Startup Expenses		3250
Total Startup Expenses		4350

Starting a Small Business

Personal Balance Sheet for TechServ Owner

A. Assets			
1. **Current Assets**			
Cash	2800		
Checking Account	450		
Savings Account	3700		
Bonds	4500		
Other			
Sub-Total		11450	
2. **Fixed Assets**			
Real Estate (home)	165000		
Automobiles	9000		
410 K	12500		
Tools/Computers	3500		
Furniture	2900		
Other			
Sub-Total		192900	
3. **Total Assets**			204350
B. **Liabilities**			
1. **Current Liabilities**			
Credit Cards	1850		
Utilities	275		
Other			
Sub-Total		2125	
2. **Long Term Liabilities**			
Real Estate Mortgage	128000		
Automobiles	1500		
Other			
Sub-Total		129500	
3. **Total Liabilities**			131625
C. **Net Worth (A.3 - B.3)**			72725

TechServ Balance Sheet

A. Assets			
1. Current Assets			
Cash	5000		
Checking Account			
Other			
Sub-Total		5000	
2. Fixed Assets			
Tools/computers			
Computers			
Sub-Total		0	
3. Total Assets			5000
B. Liabilities			
1. Current Liabilities			
Credit Cards			
Other			
Sub-Total		0	
2. Long Term Liabilities			
Sub-Total		0	
3. Total Liabilities			0
C. Net Worth (A.3 - B.3)			5000

The Financial Model	10

Introduction

Are you ready to make an educated judgment regarding sales projections, revenues, expenses and expected profits? Even with the information gained through this step-by-step process, the task of estimating sales volumes and expenses is still *fraught with the possibility of substantial miscalculations.* That is why it is useful to make at least two projections. The first one represents your "best guess", and the second is a more conservative "drop-dead" scenario. Your "best guess" represents a realistic, "guardedly optimistic" view of the future. Your "drop-dead" scenario represents the minimum financial results you must achieve to survive as a business. Although it may be distressing to consider the circumstances that would put you at the brink of failure, it is best to identify that threshold.

We are going to plot these projections on the Financial Model. The Financial Model is a single page spreadsheet that combines sales projections by volume, type and price with the normal income/expense statement. The reason for combining these two projections on one page is to make it easier to see the impact of sales on total revenues, expenses and profits. It will also make it easier to see growth or decline and the impact of seasonal fluctuations. These critical business conditions are often portrayed on different pages of different financial projections. That makes it more difficult to visualize <u>what</u> is happening and <u>why</u> it is happening. These are not separate topics; they are integrated parts of the basic financial model of the business.

Understanding the Financial Model

The Financial Model is *the* most important financial projection because it reveals the "bottom line". Are you going to make or lose money? You can't survive for very long if you are losing money. The Financial Model reflects the soundness of the business concept and market opportunity that you described in the Concept Model. If the concepts were well defined and realistic, the business should show a profit over time. If they were not, it will show a loss.

Starting a Small Business

Take a brief look at the blank Financial Model below. It is an excerpt from the TechServ Financial Model at the end of this chapter. We will use six months to demonstrate how to complete the model. We're going to start at the top left with projections of the price of average product and service packages, and sales volumes.

	Jan	Feb	Mar	Apr	May	Jun
Sources of Income						
Product 1 sales @ $ / sale						
Product 2 sales @ $ / sale						
Product 3 sales @ $ / sale						
Total Product Income						
Service 1 sales @ $ / sale						
Service 2 sales @ $ / sale						
Service 3 sales @ $ / sale						
Total Service Income						
Gross Income						
Less Cost of Goods (% mu)						
Less Contract Labor						
Gross Margin						
Expenses						
Advertising						
Auto (Mileage)						
Credit Card						
Entertainment/Meals						
Insurance						
Internet/website						
Leased Equipment						
Office Supplies						
Prof Services - Legal/Acctg						
Rent						
Telephone						
Utilities						
Salaries						
Salary Burden						
Total Expenses						
Profit before Taxes						

Starting a Small Business

Estimating Sales

As we noted earlier, making accurate sales and revenue projections presents the most difficult challenge in the preparation of a business plan. Students in my entrepreneurial course literally plead for a simple and accurate solution to the problem. Search as we might, there is no crystal ball to assure accuracy in this area. At the same time, the decision to proceed may very well depend upon these projections.

The best that I can offer is the following approach. It requires breaking down the sales opportunities into basic components and then applying growth and seasonal impact factors, based upon an understanding of your market niche.

We have extracted a six-month segment from the top left of the Financial Model to use as an example. This approach is based upon the identification of three, average size, product sales packages and three average-size, service sales packages. If you don't offer both products and services, develop the sales packages for the one you do offer. This technique works for most small startup businesses. It is somewhat inadequate for a typical retail store that may carry hundreds or thousands of products. In that case, a more sophisticated projection process that builds in a higher number of variables is required.

	Jan	Feb	Mar	Apr	May	Jun
Sources of Income						
Product 1 sales @ $ / sale						
Product 2 sales @ $ / sale						
Product 3 sales @ $ / sale						
Total Product Income						
Service 1 sales @ $ / sale						
Service 2 sales @ $ / sale						
Service 3 sales @ $ / sale						
Total Service Income						
Gross Income						

After deciding what the content and price of the three typical sales packages will be, enter the average dollar price for each package in the appropriate ($____/sale) space. For example, the price of the average product packages may be $100, $300, and $500. We used $150, $400, and $700 for the average service packages. If you did a thorough job in defining the elements of your Niche Model, you will have a good sense of what your customers are going to buy and what they are willing to pay.

Starting a Small Business

	Jan	Feb	Mar	Apr	May	Jun
Sources of Income						
Product 1 sales @ $ 100 / sale						
Product 2 sales @ $ 300 / sale						
Product 3 sales @ $ 500 / sale						
Total Product Income						
Service 1 sales @ $ 150 / sale						
Service 2 sales @ $ 400 / sale						
Service 3 sales @ $ 700 / sale						
Total Service Income						
Gross Income						

Now that we have defined the average sales packages, we need to project the number of sales that will be made each month for a minimum of two years (only six months extracted for this example). A business plan prepared to support a loan request usually needs a monthly financial projection for at least two years. You know that all of your sales will not be at the same price. You must use your intuition and research to guess at the breakdown.

The next consideration is "how fast will you grow?" It's unlikely that you will start out at a pace that meets your expectations for six months or a year in the future. So your sales volume projection needs to include a growth trend based upon the limited knowledge you have at this early stage.

The third consideration involves seasonal fluctuations. Will the season of the year impact your business? Most small businesses are impacted by the seasonal effect on individual consumers or businesses. Some are busier during the holidays, some are slower during the holidays; some are busier or slower during the summer. What did you anticipate on your Niche Model?

Now its time to merge the sales package breakdowns, the growth you expect over time, and the seasonal impact data. Not easy, is it? Some of my students say, "We can't do it". I tell them "you must do it, - it goes along with being in business". Let's look at the first few months of our abbreviated example.

	Jan	Feb	Mar	Apr	May	Jun
Sources of Income						
Product 1 sales @ $ 100 / sale	2	2	4	6	6	4
Product 2 sales @ $ 300 / sale	2	2	2	2	2	2
Product 3 sales @ $ 500 / sale	0	1	1	2	2	1
Total Product Income						
Service 1 sales @ $ 150 / sale	1	1	1	1	1	1
Service 2 sales @ $ 400 / sale	1	2	2	2	2	2
Service 3 sales @ $ 700 / sale	0	1	1	1	2	1
Total Service Income						
Gross Income						

In this example, you will note that we gradually increased sales volumes over the first five months, and then reduced them in June because we thought that the demand would be less during the summer season.

Gross Income

We now have the sales data to calculate Product Income, Service Income and Gross Income. Multiplying the number of sales per month by the specified price and adding them up produces the totals.

	Jan	Feb	Mar	Apr	May	Jun
Sources of Income						
Product 1 sales @ $ 100 / sale	2	2	4	6	6	4
Product 2 sales @ $ 300 / sale	2	2	2	2	2	2
Product 3 sales @ $ 500 / sale	0	1	1	2	2	1
Total Product Income	800	1300	1500	2200	2200	1500
Service 1 sales @ $ 150 / sale	1	1	1	1	1	1
Service 2 sales @ $ 400 / sale	1	2	2	2	2	2
Service 3 sales @ $ 700 / sale	0	1	1	1	2	1
Total Service Income	550	1650	1650	1650	2350	1650
Gross Income	1350	2950	3150	3850	4550	3150

This technique for estimating sales volumes and income is a useful learning exercise and a valuable point of reference as you start your business. Your actual sales experience will form the basis for more accurate predictions as time passes, but these initial projections can be used as sales objectives during the early months of the business. Keep your notes that reflect the logic behind these assumptions for reference in your business plan.

Starting a Small Business

Cost of Goods

Carrying our example a little further, it is normal accounting procedure to deduct the cost of goods (products) sold from Gross Income to reach a Gross Margin figure on an Income Statement. (Note: Cost of Goods does not apply in a service business that does not sell products). In this case, we assume that the goods have been marked up 100% (we included the note "100%mu" on the Cost of Goods line entry). A 100% markup means that we doubled our cost to arrive at the selling price. Or, to say it another way, the actual cost of goods is 50% of our sales price. Therefore, we will calculate 50% of the sales price each month and enter that number in our spreadsheet. Then, we will subtract the Cost of Goods from the Gross Income and arrive at a figure for the Gross Margin.

Gross Income	1350	2950	3150	3850	4550	3150
Less Cost of Goods (100% mu)	400	650	750	1100	1100	750
Less Contract Labor						
Gross Margin	950	2300	2400	2750	3450	2400

Gross Margin

Calculating the Gross Margin is just an interim step in deducting expenses from income. Cost of Goods is directly related to the number of sales so it is deducted first. The rest of the expenses tend to be more stable on a month-by-month basis, except for salaries. Salaries or labor costs may vary by sales activity.

Operating Expenses

Lets do a quick review of the calculations we have made to date on the Financial Model. We started by estimating the average number of sales at average prices to compute monthly gross income. We deducted the cost of goods (what you paid for the products you bought and resold) from the gross income to arrive at a figure called gross margin. Now we will calculate other monthly expenses in order to arrive at a profit or loss figure (the bottom line). We have included a list of the typical expenses for a small business.

Expenses						
Advertising	50	50	50	50	50	50
Auto (Mileage)	300	300	300	300	300	300
Credit Card				50	50	50
Entertainment/Meals	50	50	50	50	50	50
Insurance	100	100	100	100	100	100
Internet/website	40	40	40	40	40	40
Leased Equipment	150	150	150	150	150	150
Office Supplies	20	20	20	20	20	20
Prof Services - Legal/Acctg	30	30	30	30	30	30
Rent						
Telephone	75	75	75	75	75	75
Utilities						
Salaries						
Salary Burden						
Total Expenses	815	815	815	865	865	865

Your actual expense categories may vary from this list, so just modify the list to fit your needs. The Internal Revenue Service usually accepts all of these expense categories. That means that you can deduct these expenses from income before arriving at the taxable income amount.

Let's review some of these expense categories:

• Advertising - business cards, brochures, print, radio, and TV ads
• Auto - maintenance expenses or mileage charges
• Credit Card - merchant account charges to accept credit card payments
• Entertainment/meals - for client promotional activities
• Insurance - all forms of business insurance
• Internet/website - services provided for your business activities
• Leased Equipment - payments for leased tools, office equipment, furniture
• Office Supplies - paper, pencils, envelopes, postage, etc
• Professional Services - Legal/Accounting
• Rent - space for business operations
• Telephone - local and long distance
• Utilities - gas, electric, water, sewer
• Salaries - Payroll, including owner's salary
• Salary Burden - taxes and other benefits paid by the business

There may be other legitimate expenses involved in operating your business. If necessary, an accountant will set up a list of accounts to fit your specific needs.

It is usually much easier to estimate expenses than it is to estimate sales income. Many of the expense categories are for familiar items and the amounts stay about the same regardless of the volume of business. For example, rent, insurance, office supplies, telephone, utilities will be relatively constant unless the business really expands.

Profit before Taxes

If we total all of the expenses and subtract this figure from the Gross Margin, we get Profit before Taxes. This is the "bottom line", where the "rubber meets the road". Everything else may look great, but if the bottom line isn't adequate, the business is doomed to failure. But don't give up the ship yet! A two-year projection will reveal how time and seasons impact the bottom line. Many businesses lose money or make a minimum profit during the first year but then become more profitable as time goes by. This is often true of service businesses that depend on repeat customers for success. Let's pursue the Profit before Taxes line a little further.

You may have noticed the absence of expenses on the line for salaries. Let me explain why I don't include that entry on this Financial Model. Most of the time, a small business has only one owner and no employees. During the first year or two, the business income may be limited. I take the approach that the owner's salary is whatever is left over after all the bills have been paid. In this Financial Model, that would be the bottom line - profit before taxes.

I think it is useful for owners to view the bottom line profit as their salary. They can see that both income and expenses contribute to their personal success. Ultimately, salaries will be classified as a business expense and taxes will have to be paid on those earnings. Other salary-related expenses such as taxes and benefits will also be included as "salary burden".

This is Your Budget

Review the complete TechServ Financial Model at the end of this chapter. The sequence of information and the contents should be easy to understand now. Your own Financial Model may be just as simple. As you can see, the arithmetic involved in developing the Financial Model is minimal, but the attention required to make accurate estimates is significant.

Starting a Small Business

	Jan	Feb	Mar	Apr	May	Jun
Sources of Income						
Product 1 sales @ $ 100 / sale	2	2	4	6	6	4
Product 2 sales @ $ 300 / sale	2	2	2	2	2	2
Product 3 sales @ $ 500 / sale	0	1	1	2	2	1
Total Product Income	800	1300	1500	2200	2200	1500
Service 1 sales @ $ 150 / sale	1	1	1	1	1	1
Service 2 sales @ $ 400 / sale	1	2	2	2	2	2
Service 3 sales @ $ 700 / sale	0	1	1	1	2	1
Total Service Income	550	1650	1650	1650	2350	1650
Gross Income	1350	2950	3150	3850	4550	3150
Less Cost of Goods (100% mu)	400	650	750	1100	1100	750
Less Contract Labor						
Gross Margin	950	2300	2400	2750	3450	2400
Expenses						
Advertising	50	50	50	50	50	50
Auto (Mileage)	300	300	300	300	300	300
Credit Card				50	50	50
Entertainment/Meals	50	50	50	50	50	50
Insurance	100	100	100	100	100	100
Internet/website	40	40	40	40	40	40
Leased Equipment	150	150	150	150	150	150
Office Supplies	20	20	20	20	20	20
Prof Services - Legal/Acctg	30	30	30	30	30	30
Rent						
Telephone	75	75	75	75	75	75
Utilities						
Salaries						
Salary Burden						
Total Expenses	815	815	815	865	865	865
Profit before Taxes	135	1485	1585	1885	2585	1535

As a business owner, you need a budget to make sure your income and expenses are being managed and controlled within your financial constraints. If you didn't realize it before, the Financial Model is your budget. You programmed in your anticipated income and expenses for two or three years. You should be prepared to live with those results, or you shouldn't start the business.

Now you need to take the next step. Your budget isn't going to be useful unless you know what is going on with your finances from day to day. This is where your bookkeeping system comes into play.

Starting a Small Business

Financial Planning vs Bookkeeping

We have been discussing the issues relative to financial planning for a startup business. Setting up a bookkeeping system for your business is another matter and involves managing and accounting for funds. This guide is not the place to teach basic bookkeeping or accounting skills. If you are not skilled in bookkeeping and your business requires complex or large numbers of transactions, you may need to consider contracting with a bookkeeping or accounting service. Many small businesses find it makes good business sense to outsource these functions. If you have employees, it may be even more attractive because handling payroll and the associated tax and record keeping is one of the more complex issues for a small business. Accounting services have become very efficient, so the cost may not be a serious financial burden.

Every business must keep some records in order to report revenues, expenses and profits on its annual income tax filings with the state and federal governments. The method that you use to keep these records is up to you. If you can do it on the back of an envelope, that's OK -- as long as you can support the results if you are audited! At a more practical level, most businesses need a more formal and structured record keeping system. How do you decide what is best for you? If your record keeping needs seem to fit within the entries on the Financial Model, then a fairly simple system of accounts receivable and accounts payable and a checking account may suffice. If your business is more complex, then you may need to consult with an accountant. Once your accounting system is set up, you may be able to maintain it yourself. Making sure that your taxes are filed on time is another issue. Most small business owners need some end-of-the-year help with their taxes. So, get to know an accountant you can trust when you need advice or help.

TechServ Financial Model

The following assumptions were used in preparing the TechServ Financial Model:

- The business is starting as a home-based business.
- The business will move into a small leased space in the second year.
- No employees will be hired during the first year. Contract labor will be used to accommodate overload conditions until business volume warrants a full-time employee.
- Some reduction in sales volume is expected during the summer and at the end of year holiday season (mid-November to mid-January).

The completed Year 1 Financial Model for TechServ is included at the end of this chapter.

TechServ Task Plan

No new entries were added to the Task Plan.

Chapter Summary

Let's summarize some of the key points made in this chapter:

- Establishing average sales packages and their prices is the start of the financial modeling process.
- Estimating numbers of sales by month and type, and balancing growth and seasonal impacts is next.
- Cost of Goods is subtracted from Gross Income to produce a Gross Margin.
- Other expenses are itemized by month and totaled. This total is subtracted from the Gross Margin to produce Profit before Taxes (the Bottom Line). Your salary!
- The Financial Model drives your sales goals, as well as serving as your budget.
- You will need a bookkeeping system that produces reports to determine if you are meeting your budget. If you aren't meeting the budget, consider making necessary adjustments.
- Get to know an accountant so that you can get help if you need it. (Especially at tax time.)

Your Task

Develop a two-year month-by-month Financial Model for your business.

Add entries to your Task Plan

TechServ Financial Model – Year 1

	Jan	Feb	Mar	Apr	May	Jun	Jul	Aug	Sep	Oct	Nov	Dec	Year
Sources of Income													
Product 1 sales @ $ 100 / sale	2	2	4	6	6	4	4	4	6	7	7	5	57
Product 2 sales @ $ 300 / sale	2	2	2	2	2	2	2	2	2	2	2	1	23
Product 3 sales @ $ 500 / sale	0	1	1	2	2	1	1	2	3	3	3	2	21
Total Product Income	800	1300	1500	2200	2200	1500	1500	2000	2700	2800	2800	1800	23100
Service 1 sales @ $ 150 / sale	1	1	1	1	1	1	1	1	1	1	1	1	12
Service 2 sales @ $ 400 / sale	1	2	2	2	2	2	2	4	4	6	6	2	35
Service 3 sales @ $ 700 / sale	0	1	1	1	2	1	1	2	2	3	4	2	20
Total Service Income	550	1650	1650	1650	2350	1650	1650	3150	3150	4650	5350	2350	29800
Gross Income	1350	2950	3150	3850	4550	3150	3150	5150	5850	7450	8150	4150	52900
Less Cost of Goods (100% mu)	400	650	750	1100	1100	750	750	1000	1350	1400	1400	900	11550
Less Contract Labor													
Gross Margin	950	2300	2400	2750	3450	2400	2400	4150	4500	6050	6750	3250	41350
Expenses													
Advertising	50	50	50	50	50	50	75	75	75	75	75	75	750
Auto (Mileage)	300	300	300	300	300	300	350	350	350	350	350	350	3900
Credit Card				50	50	50	50	50	50	50	50	50	450
Entertainment/Meals	50	50	50	50	50	50	50	50	50	50	50	50	600
Insurance	100	100	100	100	100	100	100	100	100	100	100	100	1200
Internet/website	40	40	40	40	40	40	40	40	40	40	40	40	480
Leased Equipment	150	150	150	150	150	150	150	150	150	150	150	150	1800
Office Supplies	20	20	20	20	20	20	20	20	20	20	20	20	240
Prof Services - Legal/Acctg	30	30	30	30	30	30	30	30	30	30	30	30	360
Rent													
Telephone	75	75	75	75	75	75	75	75	75	75	75	75	900
Utilities													
Salaries													
Salary Burden													
Total Expenses	815	815	815	865	865	865	940	940	940	940	940	940	10680
Profit before Taxes	135	1485	1585	1885	2585	1535	1460	3210	3560	5110	5810	2310	30670

The Cash Flow Statement	

Introduction

The Cash Flow Statement reflects the actual timing of the receipt of cash and the disbursement of funds during the month. In comparison, the Financial Model projects sales themselves, as compared to when the payments for those sales are actually received and when expenses are scheduled to be paid.

Let's discuss these two financial planning reports a little further to make sure we understand each one. The Financial Model reflects all of the income sources and expenses. It includes a projection of the type, price and volume of sales. Those are all essential parts of a marketing plan. However, it is also extremely valuable for projections to be made in relation to the expenses of operating the business. This is the financial projection that produces the "bottom line" - will the company make or lose money if the projections are realized?

Understanding Cash Flow

The Cash Flow Statement is another view of the Financial Model, but it focuses on when *sales income is actually received* and when *bills are actually paid*. If you have had a job that paid you on a bi-weekly or monthly basis, you can understand this concept. If you look at when you earned the money ("made the sale"), it was not at the same time that you received the paycheck. You earned the money (made the sale) weeks before. At the same time, you receive bills for purchases made weeks or months before, but you may not pay them until the end of the month, until next month, or spread over several months. This is the concept of the Cash Flow Statement. It shows when you plan to receive the payment for the work performed - it may not coincide with when you made the sale and performed the work. It also indicates when you plan to pay your bills. Even if the sales payment is delayed, you may still need to pay for the products you supplied, as well as the other bills that have become due in the meantime.

Starting a Small Business

The real reason for doing a Cash Flow Statement is to project when payments will be received and when bills will be paid in order to determine if you will have sufficient cash to meet your obligations when they come due. This is commonly referred to as cash flow. Think back to the discussion of the Balance Sheet and specifically to the Current Assets category. Cash or cash equivalents were included in that category. We previously determined that we needed enough cash to pay for Startup Expenses. We also need to determine if there is enough money available to cover any shortfalls due to the timing differences between receipt of payments and payment of bills. This is an area that is of major concern to bankers when working with startup businesses. Does the business have sufficient funds available to cover startup expenses and to cover any shortfall due to cash flow problems, because of delayed payments or the normal profitability curve for new businesses?

Starting Cash Balance

Let's review the first Cash Flow Statement we have prepared for TechServ. We have included an owner's salary to test the impact of the salary on cash flow. The real version is found in the TechServ business plan in Part IV. It's easier to see the impact of cash flow over the course of a full year than over only a few months. You will note that the Cash Flow Statement looks a lot like the Financial Model, but there are some significant differences. Let's identify and discuss those differences.

In the Cash Flow Statement, the first line indicates how much cash we have on hand at the beginning of each month. In the first month, we will post the amount of cash that we have available to open for business - probably deposited in our business checking and savings accounts. In the case of TechServ, the owner transferred $2500 cash from his personal accounts into a business checking account.

The next line is titled "Plus Sales Income" and it is blank. This is where the decision process comes into play again for each business. If you refer back to the Financial Model for January, it shows Gross Income from product and services of $1350. However, the owner has decided that his terms of payment will be "payable without penalty within 30 days". Given those terms of payment, he will not receive the payment until sometime during the following month. Therefore, he will not receive the January sales income until sometime in February at the earliest. As a result, we will not show any sales income in January (our first month in business). The impact of this decision will become apparent when we look at the Ending Cash balance.

Starting a Small Business

Impact of Offering Credit on Cash Flow

One issue for you to decide is whether you are in a position to offer credit, even if it's only for 30 days, or must you operate on a payment-on-delivery basis? If you operate on this basis, there will be no lag between sales and receipt of payment and this is obviously the most advantageous cash flow strategy for a new business owner, if your customers will go along with it. These days, payment by credit card is common and is the equivalent of payment on delivery. However, if you are trying to establish a repeat business clientele, it may be difficult to impose "payment-on-delivery" as your standard pricing policy. Many businesses are used to receiving an invoice at the end of the month and then having up to 30 days to make payment. This 30 day delay in paying may be part of their cash flow planning. In any case, this is one of the issues that you must resolve as part of the financial planning process.

Now, let's continue with the calculation of Total Income. The next line is titled "Plus Other Income". This is where you post any other types of income received during the month, or any additional infusion of funding from personal or other sources.

Total Cash Available

Adding these three lines together produces a Total Cash Available for This Month line. This total is $2,500 since we did not make any additions for Sales or Other Income this month.

Testing the Impact of Inserting Owners Salary

When we developed the TechServ Financial Model, we made a point of not entering the owner's salary. We said that the owner got what was left after paying all of the bills - the bottom line. However, if there is a cash shortage, then one solution is for the owner to defer taking a salary. To illustrate the impact that taking a $2,000 salary each month would have on the TechServ financial results, check the Ending Cash Balance for each month. In several of the months, the cash balance is negative - there is not enough cash available to pay the bills *and* the salary. Therefore, in his final business plan version, the owner has decided to forego his salary in the early months. The only alternative would be an infusion of more cash. This example points out that the Financial Model alone is not an adequate tool for measuring the short-term financial strength of the business.

Ending Cash Balance

To determine the Ending Cash Balance we will make deductions from that cash balance total. We added the Cost of Goods ($400) with the Total Expenses amount including the owner's $2,000 salary and we have total expenses of $3215. When we subtract this amount from the $2500 cash balance we get a negative cash flow of $715 in January. The negative amount grows for several months and does not become positive until December. This is obviously not a workable financial plan. That is why the owner decided to forgo a salary for the first three months.

The impact of <u>not</u> receiving the sales income during the month the sales were made is obvious. If the $1350 had been received in January instead of February, the situation would have been better, but still would not have been workable. It is important to appreciate how cash flow works and to make sure you are going to have enough cash to cover any short-term deficiencies.

Chapter Summary

Let's summarize some of the key points made in this chapter:

- Cash Flow measures the actual receipt of cash from sales and other sources and the expenditure of cash for bills.
- Cash Flow does not measure profitability; the Financial Model measures profitability.
- The Cash Flow statement illustrates the timing of income and expenses. In some cases, the result will resemble the Financial Model, and in other cases, it will not.
- A Cash Flow Statement will be required as part of a lending package.
- The owner may have to forego a salary if cash flow is a problem.

Your Task

Develop a Cash Flow Statement for your business.

Add entries to your Task Plan

Starting a Small Business

TechServ Cash Flow Statement - Year 1

	Jan	Feb	Mar	Apr	May	Jun	Jul	Aug	Sep	Oct	Nov	Dec
Beginning Cash Balance	2500	-715	-2830	-3445	-4260	-4375	-3440	-3980	-4770	-3910	-2400	710
Plus Sales Income		1350	2950	3150	3850	4550	3150	3150	5150	5850	7450	8150
Plus Other Income												
Total Cash Available	2500	635	120	-295	-410	175	-290	-830	380	1940	5050	8860
Less Cost of Goods (COG)	400	650	750	1100	1100	750	750	1000	1350	1400	1400	900
Less Contract Labor												
Less Other Expenses												
Advertising	50	50	50	50	50	50	75	75	75	75	75	75
Auto (Mileage)	300	300	300	300	300	300	350	350	350	350	350	350
Credit Card				50	50	50	50	50	50	50	50	50
Entertainment/Meals	50	50	50	50	50	50	50	50	50	50	50	50
Insurance	100	100	100	100	100	100	100	100	100	100	100	100
Internet/website	40	40	40	40	40	40	40	40	40	40	40	40
Leased Equipment	150	150	150	150	150	150	150	150	150	150	150	150
Office Supplies	20	20	20	20	20	20	20	20	20	20	20	20
Prof Services - Legal/Acctg	30	30	30	30	30	30	30	30	30	30	30	30
Rent												
Telephone	75	75	75	75	75	75	75	75	75	75	75	75
Utilities												
Salaries	2000	2000	2000	2000	2000	2000	2000	2000	2000	2000	2000	2000
Salary Burden												
Total COG and Expenses	3215	3465	3565	3965	3965	3615	3690	3940	4290	4340	4340	3840
Ending Cash Balance	-715	-2830	-3445	-4260	-4375	-3440	-3980	-4770	-3910	-2400	710	5020

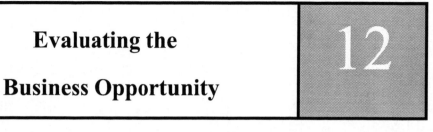

Introduction

If you have completed the three Models, the Task Plan and the other financial reports prior to actually starting the business, you have much valuable information at your fingertips as you begin the process of evaluating your business idea.

Validating Your Models

The best method for performing the evaluation is to place the three Models and the Task Plan on a table and begin to verify each item on each model in sequence from the first item on the Concept Model to the last item on the Financial Model. Double-check the accuracy of the information and verify the underlying assumptions to ensure they reflect your best view at this point in time. You should also try to validate the impact on the other elements.

Concept Model	Niche Model	Financial Model	Task Plan

Performing this step should confirm how important it is to assemble all of the critical business planning data on a few pages and in a readily understandable format. Assembling the data on one-page models is the key to this final analytical process.

Seven Steps to Evaluate Your Idea

Try using the following steps to validate the completeness of your planning efforts. The last step is the final judgment - should you proceed with the initiative?

Step 1

Review the content of the Concept Model. Should any part of the original draft be updated to reflect later research, analysis and decisions? Have you made a decision about your legal form and your business name? Do your goals or strategies need revision to meet the realities of the business environment? Have you incorporated the impact of your strategies in the Financial Model?

Step 2

Review the content of your Niche Model. Are your products and services clearly defined? Do you have a precise ideal customer profile that you can match to your products and services? Do these customers have the ability and desire to pay for your products and services? Does your pricing policy fit comfortably within the elements of your competitive edge? Do you feel confident about your competitive edge? Have you selected an advertising scheme that fits within the parameters of your promotion and sales approach and stays within budget? Do you have the attributes to build a great "bridge"?

Step 3

Have you listed all of the major pre-startup and post-startup tasks on your Task Plan? Can you accomplish these tasks within the appropriate time frames with the resources you have available? If not, how much additional time or other kinds of resources will be required?

Step 4

Have you prepared a Financial Plan month-by-month for at least two years? Do your sales and income projections reflect a reasonable growth pattern and incorporate any seasonal constraints that are factors in your industry segment? Have you incorporated the financial impact of all of the implementation Tasks in your Financial Model?

Step 5

Do you have sufficient cash reserves available to pay startup expenses and to meet any negative cash flow situations during the first two years? If not, are you prepared to seek out a lender to help with the shortfall?

Step 6

After reviewing all of your planning materials, are you satisfied with your planning effort? Do you feel you are ready to make a decision about proceeding with the initiative? Would your plans for the business meet the test of a lender as having a reasonable chance of success? Do you understand the potential risks and rewards?

Step 7

If you are satisfied that you have defined a business with a reasonable chance of success when viewed through the eyes of a prudent businessperson, what should you do next? In most cases, the answer is to develop a formal business plan. The next chapter contains a sample business plan for TechServ, LLC. It can serve as a guide for you. It is formatted to simplify the transfer of information from your planning documents.

SWOT Analysis

The SWOT Analysis is another analytical tool commonly used in the business community to assist in assessing a business in relation to other competitive businesses. It is a quick way to look at the current environment as well as what the future may hold. It fits into this planning process very well because by this point in time you have performed the analysis and definition of the business and are ready to do a business plan. This is another test you could apply to your business venture. The SWOT worksheet is found on the following page.

It is very simple to use. First you list your business strengths. They should be clear to you as a result of defining your competitive edge. Next you enter your business weaknesses in comparison to your competition. These weaknesses should also be familiar to you by now from prior research.

The final two factors are an attempt to look into the future and see what opportunities and threats may lie ahead. This sometimes has more application in an existing business than in a new business. However, it is still a useful exercise. What opportunities do you see that may develop as time passes? Part of the planning for opportunities is to be prepared to capitalize on the opportunity when it surfaces. Finally, look for future threats that may endanger your business. Again, you need to recognize these threats in time to mitigate them.

Starting a Small Business

Business strengths are on the left and weaknesses are on the right. So the left quadrants are good and the right quadrants may represent trouble.

SWOT Analysis

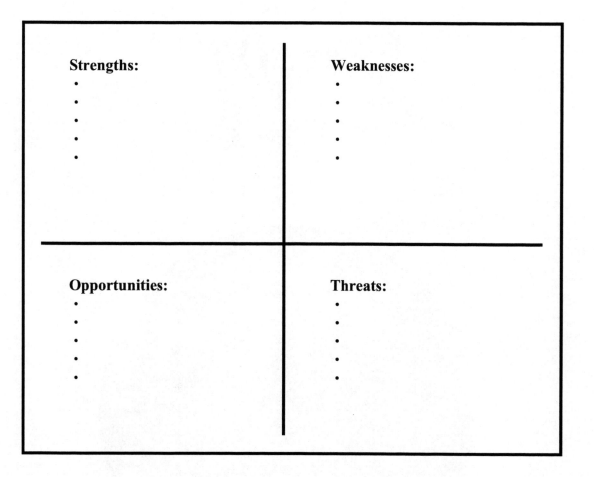

Strengths:
-
-
-
-
-

Weaknesses:
-
-
-
-
-

Opportunities:
-
-
-
-
-

Threats:
-
-
-
-
-

← **Positive/Negative** →

Part IV:
Business Plan

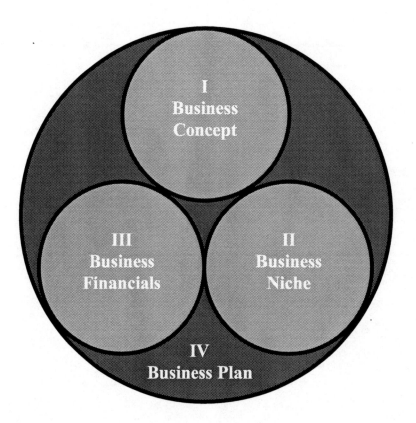

Starting a Small Business

Introduction

The graphic on the preceding page depicts the concepts and process used in this guide. The whole dark circle represents all of the information required for a formal business plan. The three lighter circles represent the information contained in the three models. The business plan integrates the content from these three models into a complete picture of the business by supplementing the data from the models with other data developed during the planning process. This additional data fills in the gaps around the three models to present a complete view of all of the business issues.

About the Sample Business Plan

This chapter contains the sample business plan created for TechServ, LLC, our fictitious company. The purpose of including a business plan for TechServ is to demonstrate how easy it is to transfer the information from the three Models, the Task Plan and the other financial reports into a well-organized business plan. The business plan provides the opportunity to expand upon the model data so that a more comprehensive view of the business is presented. However, the objective is not to create *volume*; it is to create more definition and understanding. Likewise, the business plan is not an exercise in creative writing - keep it simple, understandable and to the point.

Let's summarize some of the thought processes, decisions and assumptions that Mr. Bodine incorporated into his business plan.

- He started testing the possibility of having his own business on a part-time basis.
- He will start as a home-based business and then move to a small leased space in the second year.
- He determined that a Limited Liability Company would provide the legal protection and options that fit his needs.
- He plans to use contract labor to handle overload conditions until he needs a full-time employee.
- He decided to open as a full-time business in January.
- He will fund the start of business from his personal assets.

Compare the content and flow of the information within the models to that of the sample business plan. Moving from a concept view to a more detailed niche view and finally to a detailed financial view really works!

Business Plan

for

TechServ, LLC

Sample Business Plan for a Fictitious Company

Starting a Small Business

1. Executive Summary

TechServ, LLC is registered in Maryland as a Limited Liability Company and is solely owned by Robert T. Bodine. The business is located at 1244 W. Milton Street, Columbia, Maryland.

The business concept is to create a full-service information technology business that meets the technical support needs of business customers in the metropolitan area. We will provide information technology products and services, primarily to the small and mid-sized business segment. Our product line will include a variety of high-quality computer and peripheral products compatible with standard industry specifications. Our services will focus on the installation, maintenance, repair or replacement of the most commonly used information technology hardware and software.

We are confident that there is a market opportunity for the business, with space available within the specific niche of customers we expect to serve. The needs of these business customers are not being completely satisfied by vendors in our target community. Many of the small to mid-sized businesses are ill-equipped to handle their own information technology problems when they have breakdowns or require upgrades and additions. We expect to have a competitive advantage based upon excellent products, quality service, responsiveness and price.

As a service business, we know that our reputation will be based on the quality of the products we provide and the service we deliver. Although price is an important customer consideration, we cannot compromise on the quality of our products or services in order to reap any short-term advantage.

We believe that our goals are clearly defined and attainable. They are directed toward establishing and stabilizing the business while beginning the process of creating repeat business through quality work and excellent products at a very competitive price. Our strategies are designed to achieve these long-term business imperatives. The business is starting as a one-person, home-based business, but if our plans materialize, we will grow, expand the business and move to commercial space during the second year.

The owner, John Bodine is well qualified to manage and operate the new business. He has a computer science degree and has been working for a firm that supplies these same kinds of products and services for the past five years. During this employment, he performed primarily as a service technician. However, he also periodically acted as a sales representative by making cold calls and closing sales. On a previous job as a system developer, he supervised several junior staff members. This supervisory experience will help when he begins to add employees.

Financially we are well positioned with a personal net worth of $72,725 and an excellent credit record. Mrs. Bodine's income will provide stability during the startup period, so our financial position is secure.

We have sufficient personal funds to cover the $4,350 for startup expenses and any first-year negative cash flow periods. Our first-year financial report estimates profit before taxes at $30,670. This profit is before paying any owner salary. It appears from our cash flow statement that the owner will be able to draw the programmed $18,000 in salary the first year and still have some retained funds.

We will use our financial model projections as our first-year budget. We expect our second year will produce greater sales and increased profitability.

2. Business Concept and Market Opportunity

Our business concept is to create a full-service, information technology business to meet the technical support needs of business customers in the metropolitan area. TechServ will provide information technology products and services, primarily to the small and mid-sized business segment. We will install, maintain, repair or replace all of the commonly used information technology hardware and software. We will sell a variety of high-quality products compatible with standard industry specifications.

Our belief that there is space in the marketplace results from personal experience working for a business that delivers similar products and services. There is a growing need for these products and services as the use of information technology expands in all segments of the marketplace. Most small-to-mid-sized businesses are ill equipped to handle their own information technology problems when they have breakdowns or require upgrades and additions. Our business concept is similar to most other competitive businesses in this industry segment, except in two areas. TechServ will be motivated by a long-term view that focuses on establishing customer relationships that produce repeat business. As we grow and add employees, we expect to have a better-trained and more customer-oriented staff. We feel that repeat business generated by superior quality is the key strategy for growing our business over time.

3. Goals and Strategies

Our goals and strategies must always focus on building a business that will be successful in a competitive and changing environment. We know that technologies change in complexity and customer needs and expectations change over time. We believe that our success will be dependent upon establishing a loyal customer base and always being positioned to meet or exceed their current technology needs and supplier expectations. Our initial goals and strategies are directed toward achieving financial stability and maintaining a competitive performance position in the marketplace.

Goal 1
Become profitable (income exceeds expense) within twelve months.

Strategies
A. Use the Financial Model as our budget and maintain tight control over expenses.
B. Minimize inventory and limit credit whenever possible.
C. Negotiate the best prices and payment arrangements from suppliers.
D. Quickly implement a marketing plan to reach known business prospects.
E. Purchase low-cost marketing media for a cold-calling campaign.

Goal 2
Build a pool of customers that will provide a source of recurring revenues.

Strategies
A. Develop a list of 100 potential business customers that have repeat business characteristics. Contact at least ten each week.
B. Develop an attractive maintenance contract that can be used during the first two years to build a base of customers even if the profit margins are less than ideal.

Goal 3
Establish a reputation for quality, honesty and fair treatment in all relationships, whether it is with customers, suppliers or employees.

Strategies
A. Implement a Quality Assurance procedure as a fundamental part of working with customers. Make follow-up contacts after work is done.
B. Make sure customers understand what they are going to receive by providing estimates as part of the sales process.
C. As we get closer to hiring employees, we will prepare job descriptions and establish hiring standards. Performance will be evaluated as work is performed and in a semi-annual review.
D. Complete customer satisfaction will be one of our primary objectives.

4. Management and Organization

John T. Bodine is the sole owner of TechServ and is well qualified to manage and operate the business. He has a computer science degree that provides a depth of conceptual and academic background in the technology. He has five years of practical on-the-job experience with a company that supplied these same kinds of products and services. During this interval he performed primarily as a service technician. However, he periodically acted as a sales representative by making cold calls and closing sales. On a previous job as a system developer, he supervised several junior staff members.

The business is starting as a one-person, home-based organization. The growth plan provides for establishing a business location in a leased facility during the second year of operation. Within two years, there should be enough business to hire a full time employee. In the meantime, contract labor will be used to meet short-term overload conditions. Several very well qualified independent contractors have agreed to provide backup assistance when needed.

Mr. Bodine is actively searching for a mentor to serve as a source of seasoned small business experience. As a one-person business, he feels it will be helpful to have someone to discuss issues and strategies with and get unbiased feedback and advice. The county business resource center has offered to help find a compatible mentor for his business.

Mrs. Bodine, who is employed on a full-time basis as a schoolteacher, is available to assist with some of the scheduling, ordering, accounting and bookkeeping functions on a part-time basis.

5. Products and Services

As a service business, we know that we will always be measured by the quality of the products and services we deliver. Our reputation will be formed, and our success will depend upon how well we do in these two areas. Although price is an important customer consideration, we cannot compromise on quality of product or service for any short-term advantage.

Our product lines include software, computers, printers and other peripherals, networking and connectivity devices, and cabling. All of these products will be of high quality and will include name brands. Our intention is to provide products that customers need, at the time they need them. We have identified suppliers that will make 24-hour deliveries, minimizing our inventory requirements.

We intend to make it very simple for our customers to receive warranty service on the products we install. Should a product fail to perform as warranted, we want to rectify the problem immediately.

Our services will include resolution of software failures, virus cleanup, hardware and software installation, network design and installation, and personalized customer training. Maintenance contracts are expected to become a staple of the long-term repeat business goal. We are convinced that providing superior service in a friendly manner is the key to expanding the business. Technology products can be supplied by many vendors, but service is the true reflection of the company attitudes and values. This will be the cornerstone of our business.

Delivery of these products and services will require continual updating of personal technical skills and the availability of the appropriate diagnostic and installation tools. We already have most of these tools as personal assets from previous employment in the industry.

6. Customer Profiles

We have developed a general profile for the customers we expect to target during the first two years. We expect to expand that customer profile to include larger customers as we grow, because we will have the experience, staff and other resources to accommodate the needs of these larger accounts.

Initially we will target accounts with the following general characteristics:
- Small to medium-sized business customers
- 5 to 100 employees
- Gross annual revenues of $250,000 or more
- Industry segments that have multiple work locations sharing computing resources
- Located within 50 miles of our home base
- Not self-sufficient in the information technology product and service areas.

Our customer profiling is based upon the "need and capability" principle. That is, identifying customers that are likely to need our products and services, and are willing and able to pay for them.

However, we will attempt to serve all customers, business or consumer, during the early period. We will need to take advantage of every source of business (as long as it is profitable) until the growth in volume permits us to eliminate the more marginal work.

7. Competition and Pricing

There are a number of competitors in this marketplace and they vary in size from small to fairly large operations. Our analysis of the needs in this market segment suggests that customer demand will grow during the next few years. Information technology is one of the major contributors to increased productivity and efficiency in most business segments today. There is no indication this trend is going to change in the foreseeable future. This would indicate that there is time and space in the marketplace for a small company like ours to establish itself as a reliable and competitive provider. As noted earlier, our success will depend upon the delivery of high-quality products and superior installation and maintenance services. These are factors that are within the control of the management of TechServ.

During our startup period, our pricing will be in the average to low range when compared to our competition. This will be possible because our overhead costs will be lower than our competitors and we may need the competitive advantage of lower price to establish a foothold in the business. We will offer especially good terms on our maintenance contracts for our early customer base to lock up some stable revenue. However, our longer term pricing policy assumes that as we establish our reputation, we will be able to charge at least the average market rate for our products and services. This is the only way that we can accumulate the financial resources to continue to expand.

8. Promotion, Advertising and Sales

We recognize that finding customers and making sales are the most challenging aspects of starting a new service business. We are well equipped to handle the technical aspects of the business. Finding potential customers and closing sales is an entirely different aspect of the business, but we believe that we have the skills and energy to build successful, long-term customer relationships. We are starting with an open mind on the subject of selling and will be quick to reach out for assistance or training if sales falter.

Starting with the ideal customer profile, we have a plan to immediately identify a list of potential customers and reach them in a very targeted fashion. We expect to use a combination of personal visits, personalized telephone contacts and direct mail to establish customer awareness and familiarity with our company. We will use our existing customer list to gain referrals and testimonials. Our website will provide product and service information as well as information on our expertise.

We will emphasize our competitive edge -- quality products from multiple vendors, design experience, installation and maintenance guarantees, fair prices, and prompt, friendly responses to customer needs and concerns.

9. Task Plan and Assumptions

Our Task Plan is broken down into the three stages; Planning and Evaluation, Pre-Startup and Post-Startup. Our expectation is that we will open for business on a full-time basis on January 1. That timetable gives us three months to complete the Planning and Evaluation stage and another three months to complete the Pre-Startup stage tasks.

Our major Planning and Evaluation tasks have been research, decision-making and documenting plans. Completing this business plan is our final validation step. All of the work to date has supported the decision to proceed.

Our Pre-Startup tasks include all of the important items necessary to open for business on January 1. Getting these items out of the way as soon as possible will permit us to focus on generating income right from the start. Critical tasks include establishing the legal structure, acquiring office equipment, obtaining the starting inventory and getting marketing media ready for distribution.

Post-Startup tasks include accommodating future needs of the business. This includes moving to leased space, upgrading equipment and leasing a newer van. We expect to add tasks to this list as we gain practical experience and determine the accuracy of our estimating processes. Our Task Plan is included as Appendix A.

10. Startup Expenses and Assumptions

We have divided our Startup Expenses into the two categories of Asset - Creating and Non-Asset-Creating expenses. We have been able to keep the Non-Asset-Creating Expenses to a very manageable level. There are some planning and legal expenses for setting up the Limited Liability Company and for reserving the website name. The largest of these expenses is for marketing media. This covers business cards, magnetic signs for the van and a starting supply of brochures.

Since we already have a van as a personal asset, there is no need for another one now. We do have a plan to upgrade the van late in the second year of operation. We will need a few renovations in our home to satisfy some operational and inventory storage requirements. A combination printer and fax machine, office supplies, and a combination of software and hardware to perform diagnostics and accommodate networking installations will also be required. The inventory items will be for stock items commonly required.

TechServ Startup Expenses

Non-Asset-Creating Startup Expenses		
1. Planning Expenses	150	
2. Legal/Professional Fees	200	
3. Licenses and Permits	0	
4. Utility Installations	0	
5. Renovations	250	
6. Marketing Media	400	
7. Checking Account	100	
Total Non-Asset Creating Startup Expenses		1100
Asset-Creating Startup Expenses		
1. Utility Deposits	0	
2. Lease Deposits	0	
3. Furniture	350	
4. Office Equipment	250	
5. Office supplies	150	
6. Inventory	2000	
7. Tools	500	
Total Asset Creating Startup Expenses		3250
Total Startup Expenses		4350

11. Balance Sheet and Assumptions

We have included two Balance Sheets, the first is our Personal Balance Sheet and the second is the TechServ Balance Sheet. Our personal balance sheet contains all of our assets and liabilities. The TechServ Balance Sheet is presented to demonstrate that we will initially transfer $5,000 of our personal assets to the business at the point that we begin the Pre-Startup Tasks. We will transfer additional funds to the business as the need arises.

Starting a Small Business

Our strongest asset is the $11,450 of cash or cash equivalent that is available for transfer to TechServ, if required. We are also relatively debt-free other than for a real estate mortgage.

Balance Sheet for TechServ Owner

A. Assets			
1. Current Assets			
Cash	2800		
Checking Account	450		
Savings Account	3700		
Other (bonds)	4500		
Sub-Total		11450	
2. Fixed Assets			
Real Estate	165000		
Automobiles	9000		
401 K	12500		
Stock	0		
Tools/computers	3500		
Furniture	2900		
Sub-Total		192900	
3. Total Assets			204350
B. Liabilities			
1. Current Liabilities			
Credit Cards	1850		
Utility Bills	275		
Other			
Sub-Total		2125	
2. Long Term Liabilities			
Real Estate	128000		
Automobiles	1500		
Sub-Total		129500	
3. Total Liabilities			131625
C. Net Worth (A.3 - B.3)			72725

Starting a Small Business

As noted earlier, this TechServ Balance Sheet is included to demonstrate that we will transfer $5,000 of our personal assets to TechServ for Pre-Startup expenses. That will reduce our personal cash assets to $6,450. TechServ will use the funds to establish the business, open a checking account, and begin to purchase marketing media, tools, inventory and other items listed on the startup expense list.

TechServ Balance Sheet (at Pre-Startup)

A. Assets			
1. Current Assets			
Cash	5000		
Checking Account			
Other			
Sub-Total		5000	
2. Fixed Assets			
Tools/computers			
Computers			
Sub-Total		0	
3. Total Assets			5000
B. Liabilities			
1. Current Liabilities			
Credit Cards			
Other			
Sub-Total		0	
2. Long Term Liabilities			
Sub-Total		0	
3. Total Liabilities			0
C. Net Worth (A.3 - B.3)			5000

12. Financial Model and Assumptions

Our Financial Model starts by incorporating estimates of sales volumes by average type and price. It identifies the cost of goods and deducts these direct costs from the sales income producing a Gross Margin. Other operational expenses are identified and programmed by month. Deducting these expenses produces Profit before Taxes or the bottom line. This bottom line does not include any owner salary deductions. The assumption is that our salary will be the bottom line. However, the salary will be adjusted to maintain a positive cash flow. (See the Cash Flow Statement for estimate of owner's salary).

We have provided a two-year projection by month. For Year One, we have made the following assumptions:

- Sales will start slowly, but increase on a gradual basis. We may have some slowdown during the summer and the December holiday season.
- Service sales will generate slightly more gross income than product sales. We see this as being an advantage because it supports our goal to make customer service a business strength. Product markup will average about 100%.
- The biggest expenses will be for auto, insurance, leased equipment, and telephone service.
- The owner can survive on less than a normal wage, if required; Mrs. Bodine's income can meet the family needs for the first year.

For Year Two, we made the following assumptions:

- Sales will continue to grow on a regular basis.
- Service income will continue to exceed product income.
- Some contract labor will be required.
- Several expenses will increase due to increased volume of activity.
- The business will lease a small office with storage space for inventory and equipment during the second quarter.
- We will upgrade our van later in the year.

TechServ Financial Model – Year 1

	Jan	Feb	Mar	Apr	May	Jun	Jul	Aug	Sep	Oct	Nov	Dec	Year
Sources of Income													
Product 1 sales @ $ 100 / sale	2	2	4	6	6	4	4	4	6	7	7	5	57
Product 2 sales @ $ 300 / sale	2	2	2	2	2	2	2	2	2	2	2	1	23
Product 3 sales @ $ 500 / sale	0	1	1	2	2	1	1	2	3	3	3	2	21
Total Product Income	800	1300	1500	2200	2200	1500	1500	2000	2700	2800	2800	1800	23100
Service 1 sales @ $ 150 / sale	1	1	1	1	1	1	1	1	1	1	1	1	12
Service 2 sales @ $ 400 / sale	1	2	2	2	2	2	2	4	4	6	6	2	35
Service 3 sales @ $ 700 / sale	0	1	1	1	2	1	1	2	2	3	4	2	20
Total Service Income	550	1650	1650	1650	2350	1650	1650	3150	3150	4650	5350	2350	29800
Gross Income	1350	2950	3150	3850	4550	3150	3150	5150	5850	7450	8150	4150	52900
Less Cost of Goods (100% mu)	400	650	750	1100	1100	750	750	1000	1350	1400	1400	900	11550
Less Contract Labor													
Gross Margin	950	2300	2400	2750	3450	2400	2400	4150	4500	6050	6750	3250	41350
Expenses													
Advertising	50	50	50	50	50	50	75	75	75	75	75	75	750
Auto (Mileage)	300	300	300	300	300	300	350	350	350	350	350	350	3900
Credit Card				50	50	50	50	50	50	50	50	50	450
Entertainment/Meals	50	50	50	50	50	50	50	50	50	50	50	50	600
Insurance	100	100	100	100	100	100	100	100	100	100	100	100	1200
Internet/website	40	40	40	40	40	40	40	40	40	40	40	40	480
Leased Equipment	150	150	150	150	150	150	150	150	150	150	150	150	1800
Office Supplies	20	20	20	20	20	20	20	20	20	20	20	20	240
Prof Services - Legal/Acctg	30	30	30	30	30	30	30	30	30	30	30	30	360
Rent													
Telephone	75	75	75	75	75	75	75	75	75	75	75	75	900
Utilities													
Salaries													
Salary Burden													
Total Expenses	815	815	815	865	865	865	940	940	940	940	940	940	10680
Profit before Taxes	135	1485	1585	1885	2585	1535	1460	3210	3560	5110	5810	2310	30670

TechServ Financial Model - Year 2

	Jan	Feb	Mar	Apr	May	Jun	Jul	Aug	Sep	Oct	Nov	Dec	Year
Sources of Income													
Product 1 sales @ $ 100 / sale	7	7	7	8	8	8	8	8	10	10	10	8	99
Product 2 sales @ $ 300 / sale	2	2	3	3	5	2	2	2	4	4	4	3	36
Product 3 sales @ $500 / sale	3	3	3	4	4	2	2	2	4	5	5	4	41
Total Product Income	2800	2800	3100	3700	4300	2400	2400	2400	4200	4700	4700	3700	41200
Service 1 sales @ $ 150 / sale	2	2	2	2	2	1	2	2	3	3	3	2	26
Service 2 sales @ $ 400 / sale	6	6	6	6	5	4	4	4	5	7	7	4	64
Service 3 sales @ $ 700 / sale	1	2	2	3	3	2	2	2	3	3	4	2	29
Total Service Income	3400	4100	4100	4800	4400	3150	3300	3300	4550	5350	6050	3300	49800
Gross Income	6200	6900	7200	8500	8700	5550	5700	5700	8750	10050	10750	7000	91000
Less Cost of Goods (100% mu)	1400	1400	1550	1850	2150	1200	1200	1200	2100	2350	2350	1850	20600
Less Contract Labor					300				500	500	500	500	2300
Gross Margin	4800	5500	5650	6650	6250	4350	4500	4500	6150	7200	7900	4650	68100
Expenses													
Advertising	150	150	150	150	150	150	150	150	150	150	150	150	1800
Auto (Mileage)	500	500	500	500	500	500	500	500	500	500	500	500	6000
Credit Card	75	75	75	75	75	75	75	75	75	75	75	75	900
Entertainment/Meals	50	50	50	50	50	50	50	50	50	50	50	50	600
Insurance	100	100	100	100	100	100	100	100	100	100	100	100	1200
Internet/website	40	40	40	40	40	40	40	40	40	40	40	40	480
Leased Equipment	150	150	150	150	150	150	150	150	150	150	150	150	1800
Office Supplies	20	20	20	20	20	20	20	20	20	20	20	20	240
Prof Services - Legal/Acctg	30	30	30	30	30	30	30	30	30	30	30	30	360
Rent				600	600	600	600	600	600	600	600	600	5400
Telephone	100	100	100	100	100	100	100	100	100	100	100	100	1200
Utilities				100	100	100	100	100	100	100	100	100	900
Salaries													
Salary Burden													
Total Expenses	1215	1215	1215	1915	1915	1915	1915	1915	1915	1915	1915	1915	20880
Profit before Taxes	3585	4285	4435	4735	4335	2435	2585	2585	4235	5285	5985	2735	47220

13. Cash Flow Statement and Assumptions

Our basic assumptions in terms of managing cash flow are:

- We will have a starting cash balance of $2500.
- We will pay our bills during the month they are received. Establishing a good credit history is part of our financial planning program.
- Payments from our customers will be received (on-average) within 45 days of invoicing. This will result in (approximately) a one-month delay in receipt of cash payments as compared to our Financial Model sales projections.
- We prepared two slightly different Cash Flow Statements for Year One to test the impact of taking an owner salary. The first version included a salary expense for the owner of $2,000 per month. With this version, there was a negative cash flow in some months that would have required some adjustments, either the deferral of some bills or bringing more cash into the business from personal resources. The second version delayed the start of the salary until April. With this version, there is no negative cash flow during any month. This is the version we have included in this business plan. However, we realize that many factors can impact both income and expenses so we will watch the budget closely and make month-by-month adjustments, as required, to stay in the black.

We believe it would be prudent to build up a working capital fund for contingencies and perhaps to capitalize on unforeseen opportunities. With that in mind, we will attempt to keep expenses less than income so that we can achieve this goal.

TechServ Cash Flow Statement - Year 1

	Jan	Feb	Mar	Apr	May	Jun	Jul	Aug	Sep	Oct	Nov	Dec
Beginning Cash Balance	2500	1285	1170	2555	1740	1625	2560	2020	1230	2090	3600	6710
Plus Sales Income		1350	2950	3150	3850	4550	3150	3150	5150	5850	7450	8150
Plus Other Income												
Total Cash Available	2500	2635	4120	5705	5590	6175	5710	5170	6380	7940	11050	14860
Less Cost of Goods (COG)	400	650	750	1100	1100	750	750	1000	1350	1400	1400	900
Less Contract Labor												
Less Other Expenses												
Advertising	50	50	50	50	50	50	75	75	75	75	75	75
Auto (Mileage)	300	300	300	300	300	300	350	350	350	350	350	350
Credit Card				50	50	50	50	50	50	50	50	50
Entertainment/Meals	50	50	50	50	50	50	50	50	50	50	50	50
Insurance	100	100	100	100	100	100	100	100	100	100	100	100
Internet/website	40	40	40	40	40	40	40	40	40	40	40	40
Leased Equipment	150	150	150	150	150	150	150	150	150	150	150	150
Office Supplies	20	20	20	20	20	20	20	20	20	20	20	20
Prof Services - Legal/Acctg	30	30	30	30	30	30	30	30	30	30	30	30
Rent												
Telephone	75	75	75	75	75	75	75	75	75	75	75	75
Utilities												
Salaries				2000	2000	2000	2000	2000	2000	2000	2000	2000
Salary Burden												
Total COG and Expenses	1215	1465	1565	3965	3965	3615	3690	3940	4290	4340	4340	3840
Ending Cash Balance	1285	1170	2555	1740	1625	2560	2020	1230	2090	3600	6710	11020

Appendix A - Task Plan

TechServ Task Plan						
A. Planning and Evaluation Stage	**1**	**2**	**3**			
1. Complete tasks in guide	··········					
2. Perform evaluation of idea		··········				
3. Complete the business plan			··········			
4.						
5.						
6.						
B. Pre-Startup Stage	**4**	**5**	**6**			
1. Form an LLC	··········					
2. Reserve website name	··········					
3. Check commercial space rates	··········					
4. Get insurance quotes	··········					
5. Order business telephone		··········				
6. Develop multiple supplier sources		··········				
7. Design quality assurance program		··········				
8. Order startup inventory			··········			
9. Order startup marketing media			··········			
10. Find an experienced mentor			··········			
11.						
12.						
C. Post-Startup Stage	**7-8**	**9-10**	**11-12**	**13-14**	**15-16**	**17-18**
1. Establish relationship with independent contractors	··········					
2. Upgrade office computers and equipment.			··········			
3. Move to commercial location				··········		
4. Lease a newer van					··········	
5.						
6.						

<table>
<tr><td>

Blank Models and Forms

</td><td>

</td></tr>
</table>

1 - Concept Model

2 - Niche Model

3 - Task Plan

4 - Startup Expense List

5 - Balance Sheet

6 - Financial Model

7 - Cash Flow Statement

Concept Model

1. Ownership and Identification --
a) Legal Form:

b) Owner's Name(s):

c) Business Name:

d) Business Address:

e) Website Name (URL):

2. Business Concept (5 sentences) ---

3. Market Opportunity (5 sentences) --

4. Goals (3) --
a)

b)

c)

5. Strategies (one or more per goal) ---
a)

b)

c)

Niche Model

1. Product and Service Offerings --

     Products

-
-
-
-
-

     Services

-
-
-
-
-

2. Customer Profile Characteristics --

-
-
-
-
-

3. Pricing Policy Characteristics ---

-
-
-
-
-

4. Competitive Edge Advantages ---

-
-
-
-
-

5. Promotion and Advertising Venues --

     Personal Advertising

-
-
-
-

     Impersonal Advertising

-
-
-
-

Task Plan						
Planning and Evaluation Stage						
1. 2. 3. 4. 5. 6.						
Pre-Startup Stage						
1. 2. 3. 4. 5. 6.						
Post-Startup Stage						
1. 2. 3. 4. 5. 6.						

Startup Expense List

A. Non-Asset Creating Startup Expenses		
1. Planning Expenses		
2. Legal/professional fees		
3. Licenses and permits		
4. Utility installations		
5. Renovations		
6. Marketing media		
7. Banking setup fees		
Total Non-Asset Startup Expenses		
B. Asset Creating Startup Expenses		
1. Utility deposits		
2. Lease deposits		
3. Furniture		
4. Office equipment		
5. Office supplies		
6. Inventory		
7. Tools		
Total Asset Creating Startup Expenses		
C. Total Startup Expenses		

Balance Sheet

A. Assets			
1. Current Assets			
Cash			
Checking Account			
Savings Account			
Other (bonds)			
Sub-Total			
2. Fixed Assets			
Real Estate			
Automobiles			
401 K			
Stock			
Tools/computers			
Furniture			
Sub-Total			
3. Total Assets			
B. Liabilities			
1. Current Liabilities			
Credit Cards			
Utility Bills			
Other			
Sub-Total			
2. Long Term Liabilities			
Real Estate			
Automobiles			
Sub-Total			
3. Total Liabilities			
C. Net Worth (A.3 - B.3)			

Financial Model

	Jan	Feb	Mar	Apr	May	Jun	Jul	Aug	Sep	Oct	Nov	Dec	Year
Sources of Income													
Product 1 sales @ $ / sale													
Product 2 sales @ $ / sale													
Product 3 sales @ $ / sale													
Total Product Income													
Service 1 sales @ $ / sale													
Service 2 sales @ $ / sale													
Service 3 sales @ $ / sale													
Total Service Income													
Gross Income													
Less Cost of Goods (% mu)													
Less Contract Labor													
Gross Margin													
Expenses													
Advertising													
Auto (Mileage)													
Credit Card													
Entertainment/Meals													
Insurance													
Internet/website													
Leased Equipment													
Office Supplies													
Prof Services - Legal/Acctg													
Rent													
Telephone													
Utilities													
Salaries													
Salary Burden													
Total Expenses													
Profit before Taxes													

Cash Flow Statement

	Jan	Feb	Mar	Apr	May	Jun	Jul	Aug	Sep	Oct	Nov	Dec
Beginning Cash Balance												
Plus Sales Income												
Plus Other Income												
Total Cash Available												
Less Cost of Goods (COG)												
Less Contract Labor												
Less Other Expenses												
Advertising												
Auto (Mileage)												
Bad Debt												
Credit Card												
Dues/Subscription												
Entertainment/Meals												
Insurance												
Internet/website												
Leased Equipment												
Office Supplies												
Prof Services - Legal/Acctg												
Rent												
Telephone												
Utilities												
Salaries												
Salary Burden												
Total COG and Expenses												
Ending Cash Balance												

"Starting a Small Business"

A Turnkey Entrepreneurial Training Course

This course could be useful to organizations and individuals that encourage and sponsor entrepreneurial education and development, including:

- Business Schools
- Adult Education Organizations
- Chambers of Commerce
- Business and Economic Development Authorities
- Business and Entrepreneurial Instructors.

If you have read and used the **Starting a Small Business** book, you can appreciate the additional value that students could obtain in a class with generous amounts of personal interaction and dialogue between these aspiring entrepreneurs and an experienced teacher/mentor. Features of the course include:

- A terrific 180 slide PowerPoint turnkey entrepreneurial training course based upon the content of this book. The book is the student text.
- Outcomes for this course have been established and proven by the author.
- The course tracks the presentation flow and content of the book.
- The PowerPoint "Notes" were designed to serve as a ready-made instructor guide. They greatly simplify and minimize instructor preparation.
- The instructor can customize the course by adding, deleting or modifying slides based upon local needs and interests.
- The design of the book and the presentation format facilitates the integration of external resources and topic specific business speakers.

The course is *inexpensive* to purchase and the cost can be recovered in the first or second course delivery. The **Starting a Small Business Entrepreneurial Training Course** is only available through StartingaBiz. For more information, visit our website at **www.startingabiz.com.** The book is also available through our website.

Also by Richard Hall

Strategic Planning for Small Biz.
(for an established biz, looking for growth)